FOUL DEEDS & SUSPICIOUS DEATHS IN LONDON'S EAST END

FOUL DEEDS AND SUSPICIOUS DEATHS Series

Wharncliffe's *Foul Deeds and Suspicious Deaths* series explores, in detail, crimes of passion, brutal murders and foul misdemeanours from early modern times to the present day. Victorian street crime, mysterious deaths and modern murders tell tales where passion, jealousy and social deprivation brought unexpected violence to those involved. From unexplained death and suicide to murder and manslaughter, the books provide a fascinating insight into the lives of both victims and perpetrators as well as society as a whole.

Other titles in the series

Foul Deeds and Suspicious Deaths in Bolton, Glynis Cooper
ISBN: 1-903425-63-8. £9.99

Foul Deeds and Suspicious Deaths in and around Chesterfield, Geoffrey Sadler
ISBN: 1-903425-30-1. £9.99

Foul Deeds and Suspicious Deaths in & around Durham, Maureen Anderson
ISBN: 1-903425-46-8. £9.99

Foul Deeds and Suspicious Deaths in and around Halifax, Stephen Wade
ISBN: 1-903425-45-X. £9.99

Foul Deeds and Suspicious Deaths in Leeds, David Goodman
ISBN: 1-903425-08-5. £9.99

Foul Deeds and Suspicious Deaths in Nottingham, Kevin Turton
ISBN: 1-903425-35-2. £9.99

Foul Deeds and Suspicious Deaths in and around Rotherham, Kevin Turton
ISBN: 1-903425-27-1. £9.99

Foul Deeds and Suspicious Deaths Around the Tees, Maureen Anderson
ISBN: 1-903425-26-3. £9.99

More Foul Deeds and Suspicious Deaths in Wakefield, Kate Taylor
ISBN: 1-903425-48-4. £9.99

Foul Deeds and Suspicious Deaths in York, Keith Henson
ISBN: 1-903425-33-6. £9.99

Foul Deeds and Suspicious Deaths on the Yorkshire Coast, Alan Whitworth
ISBN: 1-903425-01-8. £9.99

Foul Deeds and Suspicious Deaths in Coventry, David McGrory
ISBN: 1-903425-57-3. £ 9.99

Foul Deeds and Suspicious Deaths in Manchester, Martin Baggoley
ISBN: 1-903425-65-4. £9.99

Foul Deeds and Suspicious Deaths in Newcastle, Maureen Anderson
ISBN: 1-903425-34-4. £9.99

Foul Deeds and Suspicious Deaths in Oxfordshire, Carl Boardman
ISBN: 1-903425-56-5. £9.99

Foul Deeds and Suspicious Deaths in Pontefract and Castleford, Keith Henson
ISBN: 1-903425-54-9. £9.99

Please contact us via any of the methods below for more information or a catalogue.
WHARNCLIFFE BOOKS
47 Church Street – Barnsley – South Yorkshire – S70 2AS
Tel: 01226 734555 – 734222 Fax: 01226 734438
E-mail: enquiries@pen-and-sword.co.uk – Website: www.wharncliffebooks.co.uk

Foul Deeds & Suspicious Deaths in
LONDON'S EAST END

GEOFFREY HOWSE

Series Editor
Brian Elliott

Wharncliffe Books

Dedication

This book is dedicated to the Memory of my dear friend

Carol Suzy Crowther

15 January 1945–28 August 2004

First published in Great Britain in 2005 by
Wharncliffe Books
An imprint of
Pen & Sword Books Ltd
47 Church Street
Barnsley
South Yorkshire
S70 2AS

ISBN: Paperback 1-903425-71-9

A CIP catalogue record for this book is
available from the British Library

Printed and bound in England
By CPI UK.

Pen & Sword Books Ltd incorporates the Imprints of Pen & Sword
Aviation, Pen & Sword Maritime, Pen & Sword Military, Wharncliffe
Local History, Pen & Sword Select, Pen & Sword Military Classics
and Leo Cooper.

For a complete list of Pen & Sword titles please contact
PEN & SWORD BOOKS LIMITED
47 Church Street, Barnsley, South Yorkshire, S70 2AS, England
E-mail: enquiries@pen-and-sword.co.uk
Website: www.pen-and-sword.co.uk

Contents

This will print a lot clearer than proof looks

Joel Gascoyne's 1703 map of Stepney. Author's collection

Introduction

Exactly where the boundary of the East End begins seems to depend very much on personal definition. Many commentators say that the East End begins at Aldgate Pump, some that it consists of the three-square mile triangle bounded by the River Lea on the east and the City of London on the west. For the purposes of this book we will say that the East End is that part of London situated east of the Tower of London and north of the River Thames. The area most people associate with notorious crimes could be limited to Tower Hamlets, but since the 1880s the term 'East End' has expanded to include Waltham Forest, Hackney and Newham, and many people living in those boroughs would be greatly offended if they were not considered Eastenders. However, I have no doubt that the purists will disagree.

For centuries the site of many of London's docks and historically one of the capital's poorest areas, the East End has also been associated with some of the worst elements of human depravity, a place where foul deeds and murder were commonplace. The part of London that today forms what has been referred to as the heart of the East End, Stepney, was largely considered of so little importance that as recently as the early Victorian period many cartographers producing maps of London, simply left it out.

After the departure of the Romans in AD 410, one legacy they left behind in the East End, in what was for centuries after their departure to remain a sparsely populated area, was some typically straight roads. Kingsland Road once formed part of Ermine Street, the road that ran from Roman London or Londinium to Eboracum (York), and Old Ford Road and Bethnal Green Road were the exit to the ford over the River Lea.

By the time of the Domesday Survey in 1086, Stepney had a population of about 700 souls. During the greater part of the Middle Ages all the East End consisted of was the eleven tower hamlets. Everything else was fields, cultivated farmland or forest, with the odd aristocratic residence or hunting lodge sited at strategic locations.

As the riverside hamlets gradually expanded outwards ancillary and support industries and trades also expanded to fill neighbouring land, and the East End, over many centuries, began slowly to assume the shape that is familiar to us today.

Acknowledgements

Mrs Iris Ackroyd, Mr Keith Atack, Mrs Vera Atack, Mr Johhny Barrs, Mrs Jan Barrs, Mrs Joan Bostwick, Natalie Clark, Miss Cherrie Conlon, Miss Iris Deller, Miss Tracy P Deller, Ricky S Deller, Miss Joanna C Murray Deller, Mr Brian Elliott, Mr James Friend, Mr Andy Gaffey, Mr John Goldfinch, Mrs Doris Hayes, Mrs Ann Howse, Mrs Doreen Howse, Mrs Kathleen Howse, Sue Kenworthy, Mr Stanley Nelder, Mrs Eleanor Nelder, Dr Declan O'Reilly, Mr David Walker, Mrs Christine Walker, Mr Darren J Walker, Mr Adam R Walker, Mr Ivan P Walker, Miss Suki B Walker, Mrs Helen Weatherburn, Mrs Julia Wiggett, Rachael Wilkinson, Mr Clifford & Mrs Margaret Willoughby, the staff of the British Library, the staff of the Guildhall Library, the staff of The National Archives, Kew.

I would also like to extend my particular thanks to Mr John D Murray, who has assisted me over many years.

A late victorian engraving of New Scotland Yard, designed by Norman Shaw, to resemble a Scottish baronial castle, and built on the site of the uncompleted National Opera House. In 1829, the London Metropolitan Police Force was formed and moved into its Whitechapel headquarters in the area knows as Scotland Yard, the name by which the police headquarters became known. By the 1880s it was clear that the force was rapidly out growing its headquarters and New Scotland Yard was built on the Thames Embankment.
Author's collection

CHAPTER 1

Foul Deeds Through the Ages

After a pirate had been hanged, his body was cut down and tied in chains to a post sunk into the river bed, and there his body was left as a deterrent to other would be pirates, until three tides had overflowed him.

One important event that most people will have heard of came to a climax in the East End in the fourteenth century. This was when the financial burden that the Hundred Years War (a term invented by the late-Victorians to describe the Anglo-French wars, between 1337–1453) placed on the English came to a head during the reign of the boy King Richard ll, then aged fourteen. Parliament decided to impose a poll tax, in addition to the other taxes already being paid, to raise more money to finance the war. The poll tax was first levied in 1377 at fourpence a head but by 1380 it had tripled to a shilling a head, a very large sum of money in those days. There was a great deal of unrest from the spring of 1381 and various isolated incidents culminated in an uprising that summer. This major uprising became known as the Peasants' Revolt, or Wat Tyler's Rebellion, after the most prominent and insolent of its leaders. Bands of armed rebels numbering about 40,000, mostly from Essex and Kent, descended on London, burned buildings, including the Marshalsea Prison and the greater part of John of Gaunt's Savoy Palace, and committed acts of violence on those in authority. They broke into the Tower of London capturing Simon of Sudbury, Archbishop of Canterbury and Sir Robert Hales, the King's Treasurer, and beheaded them on Tower Hill.

The Essex rebels were led by Jack Straw and the Kent rebels by Wat Tyler. The King agreed to meet Wat Tyler at Mile End Green, to listen to the peasant's grievances. Mile End Green was at that time a large patch of common land spreading east towards Bow. Tyler, said to have been a hardened veteran of the French wars, spoke for the peasants and demanded an end to the poll tax, concessions on the division of church lands and an end to the feudal laws allowing the domination of large numbers of peasants. Many rebels left London after the King agreed to their demands to abolish serfdom (the personal servitude which during the thirteenth and fourteenth century lawyers had consigned almost half the rural population of England). Despite his tender years, the King had been well versed by his ministers and he had learned the art of political expediency. Richard having agreed concessions, knew, that while large numbers of peasant rebels were returning home, his army was approaching London, the threat posed by the badly equipped army of rebels would therefore be diminished, almost to the point of futility. Richard simply had to bide his time, which he did.

Another meeting took place at Smithfield on 15 June. Wat Tyler once again spoke for the peasants. However, Tyler's disrespectful and impudent manner towards the King displeased the Lord Mayor of London, Sir William Walworth, who drew his sword and stabbed Tyler. Tyler was taken to the hospital at St Bartholomew's Priory, but Sir William Walworth and a party of the King's men dragged him out and beheaded him. Meanwhile, the peasants were reassured that all was well and they dispersed. The rebel peasant army having fragmented amongst the various villages and country towns was never to be reassembled; realising this, the King simply revoked his concessions and the remaining rebel leaders were rounded up and punished. Some of them, including Jack Straw, were hanged. Although the revolt failed, it did make future governments exercise more caution regarding taxation.

In June 1691 there was a serious riot by coalheavers. These were the men who unloaded coal from the holds of ships on the River Thames, by heaving it with shovels from one stage to the next until it reached the deck, where it was weighed and loaded into sacks. Hundreds of men were employed to carry out this arduous task, but the work could be spasmodic. Unrest developed over the workers' demands for an increase in pay and over competing efforts of two groups of coal agents. These agents, known as 'undertakers', hired and housed the coal heavers in the inns that many of the undertakers either owned or ran, thus clawing back much of the money they paid out in wages. Some unscrupulous undertakers mercilessly exploited their workforce, turning the scarcity of work to their advantage by sometimes offering far less than a job was worth, in the knowledge that the work-starved coalheavers would either have to take the work at the pay they offered, or go hungry. At about midnight on Saturday 16 April, an armed mob of coalheavers gathered outside a tavern belonging to John Green, a prominent undertaker. They broke his windows and threatened his life. *Green's Tavern* was situated in the

Parish of St Paul's, Shadwell, and fronted the part of the River Thames where many barges were unloaded.

On the following Wednesday evening, 20 April, a mob of coalheavers, variously estimated to number between forty and a hundred, armed with muskets, pistols, hatchets and clubs, returned to *Green's Tavern*. John Green had been forewarned of impending trouble and in readiness had bolted his doors and shutters. He and his servants took up positions with muskets and a blunderbuss at the upper windows and on the roof. Firing broke out between the mob and Green's defenders. Sporadic shooting continued throughout the night, until about ten o'clock the following morning, when the military arrived. By that time a shoemaker, along with an apparently innocent bystander, a coalheaver and a soldier, had all been fatally wounded, and several other persons had been injured.

As a result of the ensuing inquests Green and a lodger in his house were indicted in the deaths of two of the men. Seven of the rioters were hanged later for their part in the disturbance.

In Spitalfields, part of Stepney, lived many silk weavers, the most successful of whom were Huguenots, who had fled France to escape religious persecution. Some settled in Spitalfields during the early seventeenth century but many more came following the revocation of the Edict of Nantes in 1685. To the already well established silk industry in the East End, they brought new techniques and the high quality silk produced ensured there was an ever increasing demand. This eventually resulted in an expansion of the silk industry northwards to Bethnal Green and Hoxton and eastwards into Whitechapel.

A group of silk weavers, specialists in making silk handkerchiefs, gained the appellation of 'cutters', a term applied to brawlers, bullies and cut-throats. This came about as a result of the repeated disturbances the group provoked during the Summer and Autumn of 1769. The weavers claimed that they were being oppressed by their employers and organised an extortion racket that extracted a 'subscription' of sixpence for each loom, from the master weavers. One employer 'that paid satisfactory prices, insisted notwithstanding that his men should not belong to the subscription-society, or pay such sixpences and armed his people to defend their looms against the body.' Because of this, when the cutters next assembled at their regular meeting place, the *Dolphin*, an alehouse in the Parish of St Matthew, Bethnal Green, a bloody fight resulted, during which they cut the work from over fifty looms belonging to the said master

Sir John Fielding (d.1780), the blind magistrate, who was reputedly able to remember criminals simply by the sound of their voices. He kept records of criminals who appeared before him and put great effort into breaking up the gangs of robbers who operated throughout London.
Author's collection

weaver. The cutters committed these offences even though, by an Act of Parliament, it was a capital offence for rioters to cut the work from looms. There was even worse to follow when, at the next assembly of the cutters, they cut the fabrics from upwards of a hundred looms, and during the night the residents of Spitalfields were terrified by pistol shots.

Early on the morning of Saturday 16 September, a mob of fifty masked and armed cutters broke into a house in Hoxton in pursuit of a weaver who refused to join them. Other similar incidents followed. By now the magistrate, Sir John Fielding (the blind half-brother of lawyer and novelist Henry Fielding), was beginning to tire of these repeated disturbances and warrants were issued for the arrest of the ringleaders. On 23 September Fielding's clerk organized a party of peace officers supported by a detachment of Guards from the barracks at the Savoy, to apprehend the troublemakers. They went to the *Dolphin* at about eleven o'clock, where the cutters 'were assembled, to collect contributions from their brethren, towards supporting themselves in idleness, in order to distress their masters, and to oblige them to advance their wages.'

The meeting was being held in an upstairs room. When a soldier entered, he was immediately shot dead. A fierce and bloody battle followed as firing on both sides broke out, the patrons, downstairs in the tap room taking what cover they could. When the battle was over, three innocent civilians were killed, four cutters were captured and the rest had escaped over the roofs of adjoining buildings. The dead civilians had all been in the tap room, situated on the ground floor, when they were shot. One was a pot boy and the other two were weavers. One of the weavers had once been a Guardsman and survived being shot, only to die several weeks later, on 19 October, in the London Hospital, after the bullet wound he had received in his jaw, became infected. Inquests were held into the fatalities and later two cutters were sentenced to be hanged. Today there are many reminders of the Huguenot presence in Spitalfields in names such as Calvin Street, Fleur-de-Lis Street and Nantes Passage. Other reminders of the silk weaving industry are in Bethnal Green's Shuttle Street and Weavers' Fields and in Whitechapel, there is Mulberry Street.

The commercial importance of the River Thames began to take shape after the Normans established a dock in the City of London at Queenhithe during the twelfth century. However, soon after ships started leaving Ratcliffe Cross Stairs for foreign ports, the dock at Queenhithe ceased to function. Ratcliffe (sometimes spelled Ratcliff), onetime the port of Stepney, was a hamlet two and a half miles in circumference lying to the east of Shadwell in that old chaotic quarter in an area often referred to as nautical London. Ratcliff Highway (now known simply as The Highway) is a public thoroughfare whose notoriety as a place where brothels were in abundance, was added to in December 1811 by two separate events that became known as 'The Ratcliffe Highway Murders (see Chapter Three).

In *Sketches By Boz* Charles Dickens wrote:

… Look at a marine-store dealer's, in that reservoir of dirt, drunkenness, and drabs: thieves, oysters, baked potatoes, and pickled salmon – Ratcliff Highway. Here the wearing apparel is all nautical. Rough blue jackets, with mother-of-pearl buttons, oil-skin hats, coarse checked shirts, and large canvas trousers that look as if they were made for a pair of bodies instead of a pair of legs, are the staple commodities. Then there are large bunches of cotton pocket-handkerchiefs, in colour and pattern unlike any one ever saw, with the exception of those on the backs of three young ladies without bonnets who passed us just now. The furniture is much the same as elsewhere, with the addition of one or two models of ships, and some old prints of naval engagements in still older frames.

Throughout nautical London, during the eighteenth and early nineteenth centuries, trained sailors and, in times of desperate need, ordinary citizens, were often the prey of the press-gangs. Armed with a hefty expense account, the press-gang officer, would ensconce himself in some waterside inn and seek intelligence as to the comings and goings of crew members of, say, a commercial ship docked nearby. Having discovered that the crew would be drinking in a particular place, the officer would ensure that his men were suitably placed to 'kidnap' the sailors, once they had become sufficiently stupefied by strong drink. The sailors were then pressed into the service of the King, to fight in the wars against the French. Unscrupulous innkeepers could often make substantial sums by tipping off the press-gangs. Some even went so far as to deliver drunken sailors to waiting ships themselves and claim their reward.

Today there are a few notable survivors of the ancient riverside inns, taverns and ale-houses that once proliferated the East End's waterside, and during Nelson's day there were reputedly 140 in Wapping High Street alone. Two in particular, because of their associations, have captured the public's imagination, perhaps more than others. Situated at what is now 62 Wapping High Street, is the *Town of Ramsgate*. Its present name derives from the Kent fishermen who once unloaded their catches at nearby Wapping Old Stairs. It was originally called the *Red Cow*. Local legend has it that it was named after a particularly bad-tempered, red-haired barmaid, though which came first the chicken or the egg, nobody is able to explain. During the Glorious Revolution of 1688, when James ll fled the throne, legend has it that Judge Jeffreys (see Chapter Two), James's Lord Chancellor, responsible for hundreds of executions, and at that time one of the most hated men in the kingdom, was apprehended there, disguised as a sailor. He, like the King he had served, was trying to flee the country and hired a collier to take him to Holland. While it was being loaded he went ashore for a drink. He was recognised and detained. The Lord Mayor was sent for, and

The Town of Ramsgate *in Wapping High Street, dating from 1545.* The author

Jeffreys at his own request, was taken to the Tower of London, for fear of being lynched by the mob. Ill and believed to be suffering from cancer, his health deteriorated rapidly and he died there on 18 April 1689, aged forty, having spent his last weeks unable to eat hardly anything other than poached eggs. During the eighteenth century, the cellars at the *Town of Ramsgate* were used as dungeons for prisoners awaiting transportation to the Americas and Australia.

Until fairly recently, a gibbet was hung at the end of the narrow alley that runs down the side of the *Town of Ramsgate* to Wapping Old Stairs, placed there as a reminder of nearby Execution Dock, the place where pirates were executed. Up until, and during the fifteenth century, pirates were usually hanged on a gallows raised on a hill, in a field beyond East Smithfield. During early Tudor times the scaffold was moved to Wapping. The execution of pirates created mixed feelings among the local populace, and sometimes executions had an almost carnival atmosphere. The public attached a certain amount of glamour to piracy and some pirates cut a dashing figure during their often short lived careers and were determined to retain that air of glamour to the end. Thomas Walton was hanged at Execution Dock in August 1583, dressed in his Venetian breeches of crimson taffeta. Certainly the most famous if not celebrated, pirate to be executed at Wapping's Execution Dock was Captain William Kidd a popular folk hero. Kidd distinguished himself in the wars against the French and was afterwards sent to America in 1696 to clear the coast of pirates. The story goes that Kidd stated that it was more lucrative to become a pirate himself. He was captured in 1699 and charged with seizing French ships. When he was finally returned to England, Kidd claimed that he had been acting under admiralty orders, a claim that was never put to the test in what amounted to a sham trial at the Old Bailey. Kidd was not given the opportunity to speak, possibly to prevent him naming influential people who had benefited from his exploits. With no defence and two pathetic witnesses giving evidence against him, the trial was brought to a swift conclusion and Kidd was hanged at Execution Dock on 23 May 1701. There is a pub that bears his name situated in Wapping High Street between Wapping Station and the *Town of Ramsgate*.

After a pirate had been hanged, his body was cut down and tied in chains to a post sunk into the river bed, and there his body was left as a deterrent to other would be pirates, until three tides had overflowed him. Being immersed in water caused a body to bloat and pirates bodies being displayed in this way in Wapping, led to the

The Captain Kidd *in Wapping High Street, named after the celebrated pirate who was hanged at nearby Execution Dock.* The Author

expression 'what a wapper', although over centuries the word 'wapper' has been transformed through to 'whoppa', as the word is occasionally spelled, into the word that is more familiar to us today, whopper, meaning a large specimen of its kind. The corpse was then taken out of the mud, smothered in tar and chained in a metal gibbet, where the head was fixed in a metal harness to keep the skull in place as the flesh rotted away. The gibbet was then hung where it could be seen by sailors travelling about their business on the River Thames. In later years, after their execution and customary dipping in the river, their bodies were buried in St Botolph's churchyard. The last executions took place at Execution Dock in December 1830. Today the site of Execution Dock has been obliterated by Wapping underground station but other gruesome reminders remain. Immediately below the raised back yard of the *Town of Ramsgate*, right next to Wapping Old Stairs, at low tide, it is possible to see the posts to which pirates were chained after their executions.

Wapping Station, which covers the site of Execution Dock. The author

A view of Wapping Old Stairs taken from the bed of the River Thames at low tide. Some of the wooden posts to which the bodies of hanged pirates were chained until three tides had flowed over them, can be seen beneath the sign on the wall of the Town of Ramsgate. One post is partially in shadow. At high tide the bodies would be completely submerged. The line where the water level rises to can be seen very clearly. The author

A view taken from the bed of the River Thames of the Prospect of Whitby. The author

When it was built in 1520 the *Prospect of Whitby*, today, arguably the best-known East End riverside tavern, was surrounded by open fields and known by the name *The Devil's Tavern*. It soon became a haunt for some of the worst elements of Tudor low life. Smugglers and thieves frequented what was at the time a somewhat isolated tavern, and it was not an unusual occurrence for some of its seedy customers to sell bodies dragged out of the River Thames to medical students. During the late seventeenth century, this tavern was frequented by Judge Jeffreys, who before his downfall lived at nearby Butcher Row. He would often go there after watching pirates, he had condemned, hanged at Execution Dock. In 1777, in an effort to improve its image, *The Devil's Tavern* changed its name to that of a locally moored ship, which transported coal to London from Newcastle, the *Prospect of Whitby*. In 1780, the first fuchsia to be brought to England was sold there by a sailor, recently returned from the West Indies. In fact, he didn't exactly sell it. He exchanged it for a quarter pint of rum. During the nineteenth century, the *Prospect of Whitby* was regularly visited by many famous literary figures and artists, including Charles Dickens, Rex Whistler, and J M W Turner. Gustave Doré was also a regular customer and he drew pictures of East End low life here. A gallows has been placed in

(Paul) Gustave Doré (1832–83), painter and illustrator, who depicted many scenes showing the darker side of East End life. Author's collection

the river bed immediately outside the *Prospect of Whitby* complete with dangling noose, presumably to serve as a reminder of what once took place nearby.

Because of its maritime links, by the sixteenth century, that part of the Parish of Stepney fronting the River Thames had begun to assume an independence of its own. The number of ships and other vessels sailing up the river was ever on the increase and by the reign of Queen Elizabeth l, the Port of London was expanding eastwards away from the City. In 1600 the newly-formed East India Company was granted a Royal Charter and in 1614, the company opened its own repairing-dock and building yard at Ratcliffe. From then onwards the area that is loosely referred to today as Docklands, expanded rapidly. As the traffic on the River Thames increased and the population in Docklands grew, the crime rate soared. One type of criminal who reared their ugly heads were river-thieves. There was a time when the owners of craft on the River Thames practically left their back

A view of the gallows erected outside the Prospect of Whitby, *presumably to act as a grim reminder of what took place at nearby Execution Dock until 1830.* The author

An 1880s view of the River Police at their Wapping headquarters. The Strand

Plaque placed on the River Police's Headquarters in Wapping High Street. The author

doors open and invited the thieves to enter. Barges were docked holding all manner of precious cargoes, from silk to bales of tobacco. Goods in excess of a million pounds sterling were being misappropriated every year. The City merchants were at their wit's end. A partial solution to the problem was found in 1792 with the formation of 'The Preventative Service', which the early River Police were known as, until 1839, when they became part of the Metropolitan Police, with the special privilege of posing as City constables. An interesting article appeared in *The Strand* magazine in the 1880s, which gave an insight into the workings of the River Police:

... From a million pounds' worth of property stolen yearly a hundred years ago, they have, by a persistent traversing of a watery beat, reduced it to one hundred pounds. Smuggling is in reality played out, though foggy nights are still fascinating to those so inclined; but now they have to be content with a coil or two of old rope, an ingot of lead, or a few fish. Still the river-policeman's eye and the light of his lantern are always searching for suspicious characters and guilty-looking craft.

In High-street, Wapping, famous for its river romances, and within five hundred yards of the Old Stairs, the principal station of the Thames Police is to be found. The traditional blue lamp projects over a somewhat gloomy passage leading down to the river-side landing stage. To us, on the night appointed for our expedition, it is a welcome beacon as to the

The River Police at Wapping, seen here at low tide in December 2004. The author

whereabouts of law and order, for only a few minutes previously half a dozen worthy gentlemen standing at the top of some neighbouring steps, wearing slouched hats and anything but a comfortable expression on their faces gruffly demanded, "Do you want a boat?" Fortunately we did not. These estimable individuals had only just left the dock of the police station, where they had been charged on suspicion, but eventually discharged.

Many parts of London lay claim to have associations with that most celebrated of highwaymen Dick Turpin, the East End is no exception. On Monday 2 May 1737, a coachman drove into the yard of the *Old Red Lion* in Aldgate. He recognised a grey mare that was stabled there which had been stolen the previous Saturday by Dick Turpin from *The Green Man*, Epping. The coachman informed the horse's owner who came down to Aldgate with a constable and kept watch on the stable. That evening, Turpin and his associate, Robert King, were in nearby Goodman's Fields. They were not aware that the stables of the *Old Red Lion* were being watched and sent King's brother Matthew to fetch the stolen horse. Matthew King collected the horse and was followed. More help was summoned and shots were fired. Turpin escaped but Robert King received a bullet wound from which he later died.

St George's-in-the-East is one of three magnificent churches built in the East End, all in Stepney, by architect Nicholas Hawksmoor (1661–1736), the others being Christ Church, Spitalfields and St Anne's, Limehouse. St George's was built to provide a place of worship for the population of Upper Wapping and the church was consecrated in 1729. A little over a hundred years later, this church was to become notorious. A moderate form of High Church ritual was introduced by the new incumbent, Bryan King, in 1842, following the instructions of the then Bishop of London, Charles Blomfield. This subsequently brought the Reverend King into

Dick Turpin (1706–39) in his hideaway cave in Epping Forest. Author's collection.

conflict with the succeeding Bishop of London, A C Tait, who had been born a Presbyterian. Against Reverend King's wishes, the Bishop appointed Hugh Allen, a militant Low Churchman, to St George's as afternoon lecturer. Allen set about undermining King and baited him by disrupting services. The congregation were appalled and disgraceful scenes ensued, culminating in rioting. A crisis point was reached and, in 1859, it was necessary to close the church for a truce. In the end neither the Bishop nor the Reverend Allen succeeded in forcing the Reverend King to abandon his High Church principles. However, the troubles had hastened bad health and King was eventually persuaded to hand

Nicholas Hawksmoor's masterpiece St Georges-in-the East, which from May 1859 until March 1860, was the scene of the most rowdy behaviour ever witnessed in a London church. The author

over to a locum. The congregation installed a mosaic crucifixion scene not aproved of in Low Church principles, in opposition to the Reverend King's successor. Unfortunately, St George's original interior was destroyed by enemy action during the Blitz in 1941. In 1963 a new church was created inside the shell of Hawksmoor's masterpiece.

The Census Returns for 1901 show that 42,032 'Russians and Poles' were resident in the newly-formed Borough of Stepney. Many had fled from political or religious persecution in their homelands and amongst those who settled there, some were anarchists and political agitators, and there were others with high political ambitions who used Stepney as a launch pad as they plotted the overthrow of the Tsar. For two weeks during May 1907, Joseph Stalin and Maxim Litvinov stayed in Tower House, a doss house in Fieldgate Street, Whitechapel, while they attended the Fifth Congress of the Russian Social Democratic Party, held at the Brotherhood Chapel in Southgate Road, Islington and organised by Vladimir Ilyich Lenin. The provisional meetings were held at the Jewish Socialist Club, situated at the corner of Fulbourne Street and Whitechapel Road, just opposite the London Hospital. During their stay Stalin had a run in with an East End bobby, near the Anarchist Club in Jubilee Street, and Litvinov was swift to extricate his comrade from a tricky situation. A little over thirty years later, in 1939, Stalin was dictator of Russia and Litvinov had just been dismissed as his Commmissar for Foreign Affairs and replaced by Vyacheslav Mikhailovich Molotof. Fearing he might suffer the same fate as many political allies who had fallen out of Stalin's favour, Litvinov burst into Stalin's office in the Kremlin and uttered the words, 'Now I suppose I shall become an enemy of the people too.' Stalin replied, 'Whatever gave you that idea, Maxim, I haven't forgotten the favour you did for me in London in 1907.' Stalin and Litvinov have also been mentioned amongst other possible candidates as being the second ranking undiscovered East End villain, after Jack the Ripper, it being variously suggested by some commentators that either one or the other of them was none other than 'Peter the Painter', the mysterious 'Russian anarchist' who vanished following the Battle of Stepney, in January 1911.

Coulston Street, Whitechapel, the Rag Merchant's Home as depicted by Doré. Author's collection

CHAPTER 2

Foul Deeds Within the Precincts of the Tower of London & on Tower Hill

George Digby M P for Windsor (Lord Bristol's son), one of the Committee prosecuting Strafford, declared that the issue was either 'justice or murder.' He voted against the Bill and in the strongest terms told the House of Commons that it was about to 'commit murder with the sword of justice.'

Setting the scene

The Tower of London is situated adjacent to the River Thames at the eastern boundary of the old city walls and effectively stands sentinel at the gateway to the East End. Its official name is Her Majesty's Fortress and Palace – The Tower of London, which accurately describes its principal original and medieval functions. Within the 18 acre (7ha) complex, there are a total of twenty towers, nineteen being bastions, the twentieth, the central Norman keep, is known as the White Tower. The White Tower is the oldest part of the complex, and it is from that building the name the Tower of London is derived.

The Tower of London and Tower Bridge. Author's collection

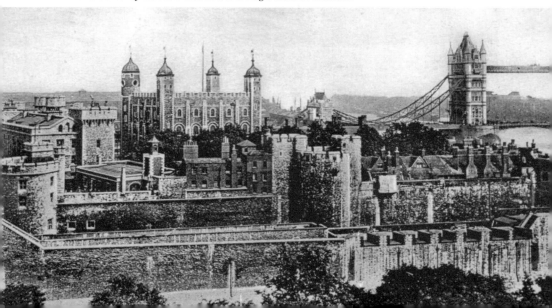

The White Tower was built by Gundulf, William the Conqueror's bishop-architect, between 1078–80. Since then, during its over nine-hundred years history, there have been considerable numbers of foul deeds and suspicious deaths within its walls. The Tower of London has served as the Royal Palace. It was used extensively as such from 1140–1625, as the Royal Mint (1300–1810) and the Royal Menagerie (1235–1834). Since 1303 the Tower has housed the Crown Jewels. The other function for which the Tower is perhaps more famous, is as a place of incarceration and execution for high profile prisoners.

It was at the Tower that Richard ll renounced the Crown in favour of Henry of Lancaster in 1399. Under its winding stairs, enclosed in the massive walls of the White Tower, were found the bones of two children, during the reign of Charles ll. These were believed to have been the remains of Edward V, aged twelve, and his brother Richard, aged nine, the 'Little Princes in the Tower', said to have been murdered in 1483 on the orders of their uncle, Richard lll, although the case against Richard has never been proven. The bones were removed to Westminster Abbey, where they lie to this day in a small sarcophagus, in Innocents Corner, close to the tomb of Mary l and Elizabeth l. From the beginning of the Tower's history, many famous people have found themselves incarcerated within its walls against their will, several of them, once having entered, never breached its walls again. Many were justly imprisoned, others unjustly.

Two of Henry Vlll's wives were imprisoned and executed at the Tower, not on Tower Hill but away from public gaze on Tower Green, within the precincts of the Tower itself. Anne Boleyn (1507–36), second Queen of Henry Vlll and mother of Queen Elizabeth l, became surplus to His Majesty's requirements after she failed to bear him a son, and he fell in love with, and desired to marry, Jane Seymour. Unsubstantiated rumours of Anne's infidelity were quickly turned to advantage, and after a series of sham trials, several nobles were executed including the Queen's own brother. Anne was imprisoned in the Tower and, after being found guilty of the charge of unfaithfulness to her Royal husband, was executed on 19 May 1536, by a swordsman specially brought over from France, who cut off her head at a single stroke.

Queen Catherine Howard (c.1523–1542), was the fifth wife of Henry Vlll and grand-daughter of the Duke of Norfolk. She married the King in July 1540. At first the King was blissfully happy with his new wife. Due to no fault of the Queen, political intrigue and rivalry between the Howard and the Seymour family caused sides to be taken and Catherine's removal was seen as a means of weakening the Howard's influence on the King. Evidence was found of Catherine's pre-marital affairs and when the King heard of them, her arrest for treason soon followed. On 10 February 1542, the Constable of the Tower arrived at the Convent of Syon, where Catherine was being held and informed her she was to be taken by river to the Tower. Following her arrival at the Tower, the following day, Catherine was informed that both houses of Parliament had voted for her death. Her execution would be on 13 February. Catherine was concerned that all should go well. She asked the constable to describe the scaffold, the width of the planks and the number of steps she would have to mount to reach it. Her anxiety extended to the block. She had never seen one and she wished that when the time came she should be able to kneel down before it with dignity. The block was brought to her and she spent a considerable time practising kneeling before it and placing her head upon it. She even went as far as to request that her women attendants criticise the attitude of her neck, such was her concern that she should bid a graceful farewell to life. Catherine died on Tower Green in the dignified manner she so desired.

In the north-west corner of the Tower of London's Inner Ward, stands the chapel of St Peter ad Vincula (in chains), a long low building, built of flint, with a brick tower, which was first mentioned in 1210 and was built mainly for use by the garrison and prisoners. It was to this spot that the bodies of executed nobles were brought to be buried. With only a few exceptions, it was just the bodies that were buried beneath the stones, as the heads were customarily displayed on pikes on London Bridge. During renovations to the chapel in the nineteenth century, the remains of over fifteen hundred headless nobles were discovered and re-buried there in several massive coffins. Some of the remains were identifiable, such as those of Queen Anne Boleyn, Queen Katherine Howard, Lady Jane Grey and the Duke of Monmouth, as they were buried along with their heads, in prominent positions, and their burials were recorded. Their remains were re-buried near he altar. Lord Macaulay (1800–59), the celebrated essayist and historian, remarked of the chapel of St Peter Ad Vincula 'in truth there is no sadder spot on earth.'

(1) The murder of Sir Thomas Overbury, 1613

Anne Turner, and a city apothecary, James Franklin, poisoned Overbury in a slow and ghastly manner, with copper vitriol.

The one undoubted murder which took place within the Tower of London itself was that of Sir Thomas Overbury, poet and statesman (1581–1613), victim of what was the greatest scandal of James l's court. He was the son of a landowner of Bourton-on-the-Hill in Gloucestershire, and was educated at Queen's College, Oxford and the Middle Temple. He served as Secretary of State under Robert Cecil, Earl of Salisbury, who sent him travelling in France and the Low Countries. Tall, good looking and extremely vain, Overbury possessed a literary talent. His influence increased after he became a friend of Robert Carr (1586–1645), a page to the Earl of Dunbar, whom he met in Edinburgh in 1601. They came to London together, and Carr attracted the eye of James l who made him his favourite and created him firstly Viscount Rochester and after Overbury's death, Earl of Somerset.

Robert Carr's homosexual relationship with the King is well documented. Some commentators suggest that a homosexual triangle existed between Overbury, Carr and the King. Overbury retained some influence over the far less astute Lord Rochester, who turned to him as friend and confidant and it was said by many at court that 'Rochester ruled James and Overbury ruled Rochester'. In 1611, however, Lord Rochester fell in love with the young Countess of Essex, Frances Howard. Overbury soon took against this alliance when he discovered that Lady Essex intended to marry Rochester if she could obtain a divorce (her husband was abroad and the marriage unconsummated). Overbury was concerned that his influence over Rochester would be usurped by the influential Howard family.

Overbury enraged both Rochester and Lady Essex with his opposition to their love affair and with the help of the Earl of Northampton,

Sir Thomas Overbury (1581–1613). Author's collection

Overbury was imprisoned in the Tower on the dubious charge of refusing to go as an ambassador to Russia, as this was contrary to the King's wishes. Frances Howard was a vindictive creature and Overbury's imprisonment did not satisfy her. Some accounts say she dabbled in black magic. Using her influence, through the agency of the Lieutenant of the Tower, Sir Gervaise Helwyss, who saw to it that one of Lady Essex's servants, Richard Weston, was employed as Overbury's personal gaoler; he with the assistance of a physician's widow named Anne Turner, and a city apothecary, James Franklin, poisoned Overbury in a slow and ghastly manner, with copper vitriol. Sir Thomas Overbury died in September 1613. Two years passed before the truth came to light. Meanwhile, Lady Essex had obtained a divorce, with the help of the King's influence and married Carr, who had been created Earl of Somerset, in November 1613.

Overbury's friend's suspicions that he had died an unnatural death were confirmed when a young man who had previously worked in the Tower fell ill in Flanders. When he knew he was dying he confessed to his share in the murder of Sir Thomas Overbury. Despite the King's efforts to keep the matter quiet, the full story came out. Robert Carr, Earl of Somerset had been supplanted as the King's favourite by George Villiers, (later created Duke of Buckingham), and the new favourite's supporters, keen to see Somerset's downfall, saw to it that matters concerning the death of Sir Thomas Overbury were investigated. Anne Turner, Richard Weston and James Franklin were convicted of murder in November 1615 and executed, but not before they had implicated Lord and Lady Somerest in the affair. The discovery of Sir Thomas Overbury's murder raised the profile of his literary works considerably, notably his poem *The Wife* and his essays *The Characters*.

For their part in the murder of Sir Thomas Overbury, the Somersets were put on trial before the House of Lords. Lady Somerset was tried on 24 May 1616. She pleaded guilty. Lord Somerset's trial commenced the following day and he pleaded not guilty. They were both found guilty and condemned to death. However, the King pardoned them and they were confined in the Tower until 1621. On their release they went to live in the country but their love for each other had not survived their ordeal. What had once been love had turned to hate. The countess died a slow and painful death in 1632.

(2) Thomas Wentworth: Murdered by the Foulest Means of All, the Sword of Justice, Tower Hill, 1641

I thank God I am no more afraid of death, nor haunted with any discouragements arising from my fears, but do as cheerfully put off my doublet at this time as ever I did when I went to bed.

Possibly one of the foulest deeds to be committed on Tower Hill was what amounted to the judicial murder of one of the most gifted statesmen England ever possessed. A man of tremendous ability,

Thomas Wentworth, Earl of Strafford K.G. (1593–1641) engraved by R. Robinson from an original portrait by Sir Anthony Vandyke. Author's collection

dignity and honour, disposed of for their convenience by less scrupulous politicians in a cowardly and dishonoroubie way, in order that they might weaken the King's authority; a crime committed by order of a dubious Act of Parliament, in the prelude to the Civil War that followed shortly afterwards. The victim of this most foul deed was Thomas Wentworth, Earl of Strafford.

Had Thomas Wentworth not been so eager to begin his life, he would have been born on his family's ancestral estate at Wentworth near Rotherham in Yorkshire. However, he was born prematurely on Good Friday, 13 April 1593, at the house of his maternal grandfather, Sir Robert Atkinson, in Chancery Lane, London. He was baptised at St Dunstans in the West, a church in Fleet Street not far from St Paul's Cathedral. Much has been written about Thomas Wentworth, a man considered by many eminent scholars to be one of the greatest statesmen in English history.

Thomas Wentworth spent much of his early life on his family's two Yorkshire estates. After attending St John's College, Cambridge, he entered the Inner Temple as a student in 1607. In October 1611 he married Lady Margaret Clifford, daughter of the Earl of Cumberland. Two months later he was knighted by James I. He sat in the so-called 'Addled Parliament' of 1614 and later that same year became the 2nd Baronet and head of the family after the death of his father Sir William Wentworth. In 1622 his wife Lady Margaret died. Their marriage had been childless.

Sir Thomas sat for Pontefract in the Parliament of 1624 and in 1625 he married Lady Arabella Holles, daughter of the Earl of Clare. She was a great beauty and an accomplished linguist, much admired at court and adored by the common people. In the first Parliament of Charles I Wentworth sat for Yorkshire. He had already carved out for himself an influential career in politics, occupying senior positions in the north of England including Sheriff of Yorkshire and President of the Council of the North. At first he opposed the King, but after the assassination of the King's favourite the Duke of Buckingham, His Majesty won Wentworth over. His considerable abilities earned him honours and even higher office. In July 1628 he was created Baron Wentworth and in the autumn of that same year he was created Viscount Wentworth, and was appointed to the Privy Council. In the north of England, as President of the Council at York, Wentworth for the most part mirrored the policy of central government, although he administered it more efficiently and thoroughly.

When Arabella, Viscountess Wentworth, died in October 1631 her husband was beside himself with grief. She had borne him three children, Anne, Arabella and William. In January 1632 Thomas, Viscount Wentworth, was appointed Lord Deputy of Ireland and in October he married Margaret Rhodes, the daughter of Sir Godfrey Rhodes of Great Houghton Hall, situated about four miles from his magnificent home near Rotherham, Wentworth Woodhouse.

Wentworth went to Dublin in June 1633. His time in Ireland and the policy he implemented there, known as 'Thorough', remain the stuff of legend, as are his dealings with the problems brewing in Scotland, where his friend and ally Archbishop Laud exercised powers similar to his own. A deep friendship arose between the two men, who were both by temperament authoritarian men of action. Given full powers, and on virtually every occasion the full support of Whitehall, Wentworth 'ruled Ireland like a king'. In six years he reorganised the country's finances, the army and the navy, and the law courts. He also brought new blood into the Protestant Church, increased revenue from customs, initiated industrial projects (which included the establishment of the Irish linen industry), and brought piracy under control. His financial policy was so effective that no subsidy was required from England; and his pursuit of Laudian policy among the Irish Protestants, enforcing discipline upon the clergy and taking back ecclesiastical land from the laity, seemed to some to pose a threat to both land and mercantile property and was a cause of considerable unease, causing a host of opponents throughout the land.

In 1638/39 the whole fabric of Charles I's government was threatened by the Scottish revolt against Laud's ecclesiastical policy. The King turned to Wentworth for help, and sent a message that ended with the words,

> *Come when you will, ye shall be welcome to your assured friend, Charles R.*

In September 1639 Wentworth returned to England at the King's request, for His Majesty required closer counsel, having ruled for eleven years without summoning Parliament. In January 1640 Viscount Wentworth was created Lord Lieutenant of Ireland, Baron Raby and Earl of Strafford, Newmarch and Oversley. Strafford or Strafforth is the name of the wapentake (division of the shire) in which Wentworth Woodhouse is situated. It is either as Thomas

Wentworth, Earl of Strafford, or simply as the great Earl of Strafford that history remembers him.

Wentworth used his influence with the king to give him the additional barony, as he had always wanted his son William to have some visible part in his own good fortune. By choosing the title Baron Raby, it enabled his beloved son to be known by the courtesy title Lord Raby instead of Lord Wentworth, as the Earl of Cleveland's heir was also known by the courtesy title Lord Wentworth. However, his choice caused great offence to Sir Harry Vane. The title Lord Raby had been forfeited during the reign of Elizabeth I, and the Raby estates had later fallen into the hands of Sir Harry Vane, who had hoped to be created Baron Raby himself. Sir Harry Vane, the King's principal Secretary of State, was not impressed by the obscure family connection with the original holder of the title which the newly created Earl of Strafford cited as his reason choosing the Raby title, and he never forgave Strafford for what he considered to be a deliberate slight. Vane had no liking for Strafford, and was jealous of his achievements. Strafford, had scant regard for Vane, who he mistrusted.

Strafford returned to Dublin on 18 March 1640, charged with the task of raising money for the pending war with Scotland. By supporting Charles I in his struggle with the Scottish dissenters, the Irish Roman Catholics were hoping to secure greater toleration for their own religion. As soon as the session had ended Strafford returned to Westminster to take his seat in the House of Lords, in the 'Short Parliament', which he had advised the King to call. When Parliament refused to grant the King's requests until their grievances had been addressed, he dissolved it. England went to war against the Scots in August 1640, and by the 20th the Scots had crossed the Tweed. Despite Strafford's protests that he was no soldier, the King appointed him Lieutenant-General of the Army, under the Earl of Northumberland. As a reward for Strafford's efforts to rally his Yorkshire supporters to the royal standard, the King made him a Knight of the Garter.

Strafford had made many enemies at court during his climb to the highest offices in the land, as exceptionally intelligent and gifted men often do. Petty jealousy and envy compounded previously minor disagreements into hatred and several former friends and allies in the Commons, influenced by the Puritans, saw Strafford as a major stumbling block in their disputes with the King's authority. Unable to pursue his policy in Scotland without sufficient funds, the King summoned Parliament.

The 'Long Parliament' met on 3 November 1640. His Majesty needed Strafford's counsel and sent for him. Strafford left his home at Wentworth for London on 6 November, in his own words, 'with more dangers beset, I believe, than ever a man went out of Yorkshire'. After his arrival in London on 9th November, his enemies, who included John Pym and his own brother-in-law, Denzil Holles, wasted no time. They wanted to remove him entirely from the scene and thus weaken the King's authority.

Strafford was the most gifted statesman of the day, and the King relied greatly on his judgement and trusted him more than anyone else in the kingdom. With Strafford at his side, Charles I had a greater chance of achieving his aims and stamping his authority on those who were rallying against him. Those who hoped to restrict the King's authority knew that without Strafford at his side His Majesty would be much easier to deal with. With that end in sight, Strafford's enemies impeached him on nine general and twenty-eight specific charges and he was committed to the Tower of London on 25 November 1640. Strafford was not unduly concerned and commented in a letter to the Earl of Ormonde: 'I thank God I see nothing capital in their charge, nor any other thing which I am not able to answer as becomes an honest man.'

On 21 January 1641 the detailed charges were brought before the House of Commons. After protracted legal wrangling Strafford's trial commenced in Westminster Hall on Monday 22 March. He acted as his own defence, and conducted the entire proceedings with great skill. His powers of reasoning, intellectual prowess, considerable knowledge of legal matters and fine oratorial skills were all put to the test, and his defence was masterly. There was nothing treasonable in the charges against him, although it was on a charge of high treason that his enemies wished to see him brought down. He stood his ground and by 10 April it was clear that a guilty verdict could not be brought. However, his enemies were not satisfied. Conventional means had failed to bring him down so they determined to take another course. An individual could be found guilty by Act of Parliament, a procedure seldom adopted to bring down a minister of the crown. Known as a Bill of Attainder, this would enable Strafford's enemies to find him guilty. (In simple terms, the Attainder enabled those who wished to accuse an individual of certain crimes to find him guilty automatically of the charges mentioned on the document, *providing the Attainder was endorsed by the King himself*. As the members crowded out of Westminster Hall, one of them, Sir

Arthur Hazelrig, a friend and associate of John Pym, was carrying in his pocket a scroll that contained the substance of the charges against Strafford, already in the form of a Bill of Attainder. Chillingly, it included the charge of high treason.

Pym was apprehensive about how the Lords would receive the Attainder but in the Commons he had prepared his ground well. The Bill of Attainder was duly introduced and began its passage through the parliamentary system. On 13 April, his 48th birthday, Strafford was brought to Westminster Hall to defend himself for the last time. He addressed himself exclusively to the Lords, giving a powerful and moving speech. Many of those who witnessed it were moved to tears. More than half of those assembled were in Strafford's favour. John Pym was taken aback by Strafford's magnificent defence and moving delivery. He had to make a reply, which fell far short of Strafford's performance. Despite rejoicing in the Strafford camp, Pym was unperturbed. He remained steadfast in his resolve to destroy Strafford.

The Commons debated the bill against Strafford. It had a rough passage and its presentation to the King was only achieved after threats, accusations and every conceivable kind of underhandedness had been exercised against members of both houses. It seems inconceivable that Pym and his supporters were so determined to proceed on the premise that Strafford was guilty even if legally he was innocent. George Digby M P for Windsor (Lord Bristol's son), one of the Committee prosecuting Strafford, declared that the issue was either 'justice or murder.' He voted against the Bill and in the strongest terms told the House of Commons that it was about to 'commit murder with the sword of justice.'

The House of Commons passed the Bill of Attainder against the Earl of Strafford on 21 April, by a majority of 204 to 59. In breach of parliamentary privilege the names of those who had voted against the bill were posted up throughout London, with the caption 'These are the Straffordians, betrayers of their country.' Two thousand citizens of London invaded Parliament with a petition pleading for Strafford's life. On 23 April the King sent a secret message to Strafford:

The misfortune which has fallen upon you, being such that I must lay by the thought of employing you hereafter in my affairs, yet I cannot satisfy myself in honour or conscience without assuring you now, in the midst of your troubles, that upon the word of a King you shall not suffer in life, honour or fortune.

The bill received its first reading in the Lords on 26 April and was read again on the 27. Riots, threats, abuse and general social unrest were the order of the day, as Pym and his cronies strived to bring about Strafford's end. Timidity prevailed in the Lords. The whole bench of bishops took it upon themselves to decide that they were disqualified from voting. On 8 May the bill was finally put to the vote. Only 48 of the 147 peers entitled to vote took their seats — less than a third of their number. The Bill of Attainder was passed by 37 votes to 11. Now only the King stood in its way and His Majesty refused to sign it. Before, during and after Strafford's trial, his enemies had been stirring up trouble. They encouraged the mob to refer to Strafford as 'Black Tom Wentworth', the name by which he had been known by his enemies in Ireland, and assured them that all would be well in the land if Strafford were gone. Riots took place and the powerful message of the mob was that 'Black Tom Wentworth' must die.

Still the King refused to betray his most loyal subject, ally and friend. Then matters took a turn for the worse. On 9 May the mob stormed Whitehall Palace and threats were made against the lives of the Queen and other members of the royal family. The Constable of the Tower, Lord Newport, declared that he would have his prisoner killed if the King refused to sign Strafford's Attainder. Perhaps in fear for the safety of his family, or because of the hopelessness of the situation, the King finally gave the Royal Assent and the Bill became an Act of Attainder. As the King laid down the pen, tears gathered in his eyes and he said 'My Lord of Strafford's condition is happier than mine.' With this signature, many believe that Charles I sealed not just his subject's fate but his own as well.

On hearing the news late in the evening on 9 May, Strafford replied to Dudley Carlton its bearer, 'Put not your trust in princes nor in the sons of men for in them there is no salvation.' Strafford's honours were forfeited and he was now simply Thomas Wentworth again. His enemies had got what they wanted, but perhaps even they had some scruples, for no one spoke of enforcing the law to its full limit. The Act of Attainder provided that as a traitor he should be hanged, drawn and quartered, but his enemies were content to see him beheaded. The execution was a great event for the *hoi polloi*. Over two hundred thousand people watched the event - a number which at that time accounted for the greater part of the population of London. Special stands were hurriedly built to afford the crowds better views of the scaffold. The scene is clearly depicted in a famous engraving by Wenceslas Hollar. There was a terrible accident on the day of the execution when some seating collapsed and sixteen people were killed and large numbers seriously injured. The collapsed stand can clearly be seen in the engraving.

On 12 May 1641 the crowds gathered on Tower Hill. At eleven o'clock Sir William Balfour came to see if the prisoner was ready. Dressed in black, as was his custom, he was calmly waiting with his two chaplains. Balfour, afraid that the mob would tear Wentworth to pieces, advised him to send for his coach. Wentworth declined, saying, 'No. I would sooner look death in the face and I hope the people too; I care not how I die whether by the hand of the executioner or by the madness and fury of the people; if that may give them better content it is all one to me.' As the prisoner and the execution party of officials and friends walked to Tower Hill, they passed the window of Wentworth's fellow-prisoner Archbishop

Laud, his friend and ally, who was shortly to suffer a similar fate. Wentworth knelt down and said 'Your prayers and your blessing.' Laud held out his hand, but was overcome with grief and fainted. As Wentworth continued on his journey he called out 'Farewell, my lord; God protect your innocency.'

As the party made their way through the gates, a narrow pathway cleared. Wentworth was saluted by some people in the crowd and he walked with dignity,

A detail from the painting by Paul Delaroche, showing Lord Strafford on his way to his execution on Tower Hill, kneeling below the window of the cell of William Laud, Archbishop of Canterbury, in the Tower of London, to receive his blessing.
Author's collection

hat in hand, acknowledging the courtesies extended to him. Some commented afterwards that he walked like a great general marching to victory. On the scaffold he made several speeches. He addressed the crowd, asking them, when the times changed, to judge him by his actions. His companions had joined him on the scaffold, with various officials, clergy and those there expressly to record for posterity what was said or done. He took each one by the hand. His brother, Sir George Wentworth, was grief-stricken, but Wentworth consoled him with the words:

> *Brother, what do you see in me that deserves these tears? Doth my fear betray my guiltiness or my too much boldness my atheism? Think now, and this is the third time that you accompany me to my marriage bed. Nor ever did I throw off my clothes with such freedom and content as in this my preparation for my grave. That stock must be my pillow. Here will I rest and rest from all my labours. No thoughts of envy, no dreams of*

The execution of Thomas Wentworth, Earl of Strafford, Tower Hill 12 May 1641, engraved by Wenceslas Hollar. Author's collection

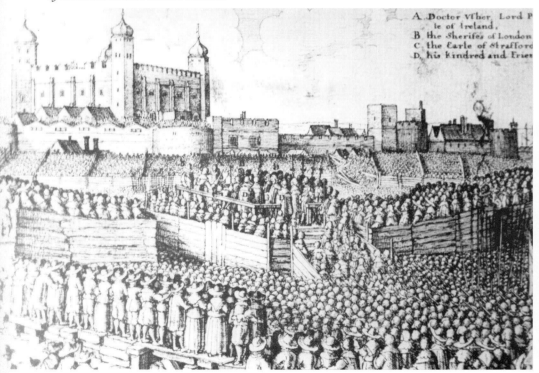

treason, jealousies of foes, cares for the King, the State or myself shall interrupt this nap. Therefore, brother, with me pity my enemies who beside their intention have made me blessed. Rejoice in my innocency, rejoice in my happiness.

He then took off his doublet and said 'I thank God I am no more afraid of death, nor haunted with any discouragements arising from my fears, but do as cheerfully put off my doublet at this time as ever I did when I went to bed.' Putting on a white cap, he called 'Where is the man that shall do this last office?' The executioner, Richard Brandon, stepped forward to ask his forgiveness, and Wentworth replied, 'I forgive you and all the world.' After refusing a blindfold with the words 'Nay, for I will see it done', he knelt in prayer for a few moments with the Bishop of Armagh on one side and the minister on the other. After first trying out the block, he finally laid his head down for the last time. Then the executioner struck, severing his head from his body with one blow. The dripping head was held up by Brandon with the words 'God save the King'. Horsemen rode out from all four corners of the scaffold to be first to spread the news, calling out 'His head is off! His head is off!' The headless body of this distinguished statesman was not buried in St Peter ad Vincula, within the precincts of the Tower, nor was his head par-boiled, put on a pike and displayed on London Bridge. During the afternoon following his execution Wentworth's head and body mysteriously disappeared. In fact, they were spirited away to Yorkshire for a decent burial. Perhaps a blind eye was turned to the removal of the body from the Tower of London. Everyone concerned with the whole affair was aware that Wentworth was executed for convenience and not for any crime.

(3) William Laud: Death of the Red-Faced Archbishop, 1645

His head was severed with one blow of the axe and held up to the crowd, his characteristic red face, now ashen white.

William Laud, who rose to become Archbishop of Canterbury (1573–1645) was born in Reading, Berkshire, the son of a clothier. His education at Reading Grammar School was followed by his attendance at St John's College, Oxford in 1589, where he advanced from scholar to Fellow and finally in 1611, President. He was ordained in 1601. Highly gifted, Laud's advancement was rapid. He became King's Chaplain in 1611, Bishop of St David's in 1621,

Bishop of Bath and Wells and a privy councillor in 1626, Bishop of London in 1628, and finally Archbishop of Canterbury in 1633. He was a member of the Court of Star Chamber. He worked closely with Thomas Wentworth, Earl of Strafford and Charles 1 in their attempts to establish absolutism in church and state. In Scotland, he met with tremendous opposition when he attempted to anglicize the Church. His ruthless implementation of the 'Thorough' policy in Scotland in a similar fashion to that being practiced in Ireland by Strafford, to whom he was closely aligned and greatly admired, made him many enemies during a time when fears of Roman Catholicism were rife and the engine of Puritanism was gathering speed. Laud unsuccessfully, attempted to combat the spread of Presbyterianism in Scotland, and it was felt in England that the spirit of religion was being submerged by rules and ritual. However, Laud's achievements far outweighed any shortcomings and his positive achievements should not be forgotten. The Laudian church attracted some clergy of high quality, including Robert Burton (1577–1640), writer, Thomas Fuller (1608–61), clergyman and antiquary, George

The site of the scaffold (within chained area) on Tower Hill. Plaques commemorate some of those executed there. The author

Herbert (1593–1633), clergyman and poet, Robert Herrick (1591–1674), poet, Jeremy Taylor (1613–67), the great theologian. Laud led a tremendous campaign to repair decaying church buildings and during the 1630's raised £100,000 from charitable Anglicans towards the cause of building or repairing churches.

Suspected of inciting King Charles to defy Parliament, Archbishop Laud was impeached by the Long Parliament on 18 December 1640, and on 1 March 1641, he was arrested on a charge of High Treason and imprisoned in the Tower. He spent a lengthy imprisonment in the Tower under the watchful eye of his feckless Puritan captors, before being executed on Tower Hill on 10 January 1645, like Strafford, also by Act of Attainder. He suffered his fate with dignity and said on the scaffold 'I have always lived in the Protestant religion as established in England and in that I come here now to die. He went on to say 'The King also, is as sound a Protestant as any man in the Kingdom.'. His head was severed with one blow of the axe and held up to the crowd, his characteristic red face, now ashen white. Archbishop Laud's body was buried in All Hallows Church, Barking.

(4) An Ignoble End for a Would-be King, 1685

Ketch threw down the axe with the words, 'God damn me, I cannot do it! My heart fails me!'

James Scott, Duke of Monmouth (1649–85) was the eldest illegitimate son of Charles ll, whose mother was Charles's Welsh mistress, Lucy Walter. Lucy Walter maintained that she and Charles had married and she was his only lawful wife, a claim she persisted in making until her death in 1658. The Duke of Monmouth was born at The Hague, and spent his childhood in exile. He grew up in the Restoration court as his father's spoiled favourite. He was good looking and athetic. At the age of nineteen, he was made Captain of the King's Life Guard and two years later became Captain-General of the army, serving in campaigns against the Dutch in 1672–3 and in 1678, he commanded the force sent to Ostend against the French. He was popular with the London mob and his popularity was extended further afield after his victory at Bothwell Brig in 1679. A staunch Protestant, his claim to the throne was supported by the Whigs, whom his father disliked, and this caused the King considerable distress.

The year before, in October 1678, Dr Titus Oates and Dr Israel Tonge, two clergymen with dubious reputations, had disclosed a Catholic plot to murder the King and place his brother James, the Catholic Duke of York, on the throne. The Popish Plot as the affair was known, was later proved to be false but the resulting furore cause widespread anti-Catholic feeling and led Parliament to attempt to exclude the Duke of York from the throne. This further convinced Monmouth that he himself should be King, but Charles would hear none of it.

In the Autumn of 1679 Monmouth, having been stripped of his offices, was banished abroad but returned soon afterwards without the King's permission. Ordered abroad again, he refused to go. Instead of obeying his father's will, he went on a series of progresses between 1680–82 round England, conducting himself in semi-royal state, during which time he spread the rumour of the 'Black Box' , which was said to contain the marriage certificate of his father, the King, to Lucy Walter. So serious were the implications of this assertion, that Charles felt it expedient to sign a formal statement before the Privy Council of Monmouth's illegitimacy. Charles was determined that his brother, James, the catholic Duke of York, should succeed him but there was considerable support gathering for Monmouth's claim to the throne.

Monmouth's involvement in the plot to murder the King in 1683, known as the Rye House Plot, had serious consequences for him, although he was the only member of the Whig Council of six to escape arrest. He was banished from court. Following a short-lived reconciliation with his father, he fled to Holland. There he became associated with the Earl of Argyll, who had fled his native Scotland under sentence of death in 1681, for hesitating to accept a Test Act to exclude Presbyterians from public office. Monmouth and Argyll found a few supporters willing to rally to the cause of placing Monmouth on the throne, after his father's death. Charles ll died in February 1685 and was succeeded by his brother James, Duke of York, who became James ll.

Following James' succession, Monmouth, the Earl of Argyll and several supporters prepared to join them in an invasion aimed at arousing the more Protestant parts of England against the Catholic King. The Earl of Argyll went to Scotland with the intention of rallying support from Campbell lands and the Borders, while Monmouth rallied his supporters in England. Then both would march on London. But when Argyll landed at Kintyre, in May, he found his lands were already occupied by the Marquess of Atholl, who was loyal to James ll. Meanwhile, Monmouth had landed at Lyme Regis, Dorset, early in June, with a few followers. He declared that James had started the Great Fire of London and had killed Charles by poisoning him. He claimed the throne on the grounds of his Protestantism as well as his legitimacy. Leaving most of his provisions in Lyme Regis, Monmouth marched inland and had successfully raised an army, mostly of farm labourers and cloth weavers, but very few gentry joined him. Unfortunately, the supplies he had left in Lyme Regis, were seized by a government ship. In Scotland, Argyll had difficulty rallying support and he was captured on a forlorn march against Glasgow. On the very day Monmouth proclaimed himself King, in Taunton on 18 June. Argyll was executed in accordance with the sentence passed on him in 1681.

Argyll's campaign in Scotland dealt and unfortunate blow to Monmouth. It encouraged Parliament to vote money for a professional army. James had sufficient time on his side, which enabled him to raise his army. He did this, in part by borrowing troops from abroad. The Presbyterian connection of Argyll enabled the government to denounce Monmouth's army as Noncomformists.

After declaring himself King, Monmouth and his army marched towards Bristol, but were halted at Keynsham. They retreated to Bridgwater through Bath and Frome. With an army of barely 3,000 men, mostly armed with scythes and pitchforks, Monmouth attempted a night attack on the Royal army, who were encamped east of the town among the marshes of Sedgemoor. As Monmouth's ragged army tried to cross in front of the Royal foot soldiers, the rebel force was plunged into chaos. The Royal forces held their ground and in the misty dawn of 6 July 1685, the Battle of Sedgemoor came to its bloody conclusion. When he knew all was lost, Monmouth fled the battlefield, leaving his ill-trained peasant army to be butchered. He was captured a few days later, hiding in a ditch in the New Forest by men of the Sussex Militia under Lord Lumley. He was hurried to London where he pleaded with his uncle to spare his life. James remarked following his interview with his nephew, 'he did behave himself not so well as I expected from one who had taken it upon him to be king.'

Monmouth was not put on trial, as Parliament had already passed and Act of Attainder, declaring his life forfeit, for what was his clear treason. After he had mounted the scaffold on Tower Hill, James Scott, Duke of Monmouth, handed the executioner Jack Ketch, a purse, with the words 'Here are six guineas for you. Pray do your business well: don't serve me as you did my Lord Russell. I have heard you struck him three or four times.' Ketch had executed Lord William Russell, son of the Duke of Bedford, in 1683 at Lincoln's Inn Fields. He had been implicated in the Rye House Plot. Monmouth then handed his servant some more gold coins, which were to be given to Ketch if he dispatched him well.

Monmouth said to Ketch, ' If you strike me twice, I cannot promise not to stir.' Having knelt before the block, Monmouth got to his feet again and said 'Prithee let me feel the ax' Having done so he said to Ketch 'I fear it is not sharp enough.'

Monmouth knelt once again and placed his head on the block. He dropped a handkerchief as a signal to Ketch that he should strike. Ketch swung the axe through the air and dealt Monmouth a blow that caused him only superficial harm. As the Duke's head moved under the blow, he gave Ketch a look of disdain. Two more blows of the axe followed but the Duke's head was still attached to his body. Ketch threw down the axe with the words, 'God damn me, I cannot do it! My heart fails me!' The Sheriff, whose responsibility it was to see the execution was carried out, barked out an order to Ketch 'Take up the ax, man! Take up the ax!' The crowd were wild with fury. They had not come to see Monmouth butchered. Having picked up the axe again, Ketch swung it through the air and struck the neck of the hapless Duke twice more but still the head remained attached to the body. Five blows of the axe could not do the job, and finally the Duke's head was removed only after the last sinews were cut through with a knife by Ketch, who narrowly escaped being lynched by the angry mob. Following his execution the Duke of Monmouth's remains were buried under the altar, close to Queen Anne Bolyn and Queen Catherine Howard, in the church of St Peter Ad Vincular, within the precincts of the Tower of London.

Lord Chief Justice Jeffreys (1648–89).
Author's collection

Many of Monmouth's followers were to suffer the death penalty in Lord Chief Justice Jeffreys' 'Bloody Assizes', which King James referred to as 'his campaign in the west.' Jeffreys progressed through the western counties during the Autumn of 1685, continuing the work of retribution and terror, which had begun in the immediate aftermath of the Battle of Sedgemoor. The Bloody Assizes moved from Winchester to Salisbury, Dorchester, Exeter, Taunton, Wells and Bristol. Hundred were crammed into gaols and churches were requisitioned as makeshift prisons. Rebels and those who had supported them faced transportation to the West Indies or to die a traitors death of being hanged, drawn and quartered. Around 300 were executed and many hundreds more were sentenced to transportation.

CHAPTER 3

Ratcliffe Highway Murders
1811

Willams was buried in a grave over which the main water pipe ran, with a stake through his heart. During the hours of darkness, between twelve and one o'clock, the body was taken from the platform and lowered into the grave and then a stake was driven through it before the grave was filled in.

The Ratcliffe Highway Murders, as these infamous crimes were known, rank amongst the most brutal of all London murders. They occurred on 7 and 19 December 1811 in what is today simply known as The Highway, described by Thomas De Quincey as:

a public thoroughfare in the most chaotic quarter of eastern, or nautical, London; and at this time, when no adequate police service existed except the detective police of Bow Street, admirable for its own peculiar purposes, but utterly commensurate to the general service of the capital, it was a most dangerous quarter.

The first victim was Mr Marr, a young man who kept a lace and hosiery shop at No.29. His young servant girl found, on returning from purchasing some oysters for supper, Mr Marr's body and those of his wife, baby and apprentice boy of 13, all violently slaughtered, their heads smashed in and their throats cut. Nothing of any value had been taken.

De Quincey also said of Ratcliffe Highway:

Every third man, at the least, might be set down as a foreigner, Lascars, Chinese, Moors, Negroes, were met at every step. And apart from the manifold ruffianism, shrouded impenetrably under the mixed hats and turbans of men whose past was untraceable to any European eye, it is well known that the navy of Christendom is the sure receptacle of all the murderers and ruffians whose crimes have given them a motive for withdrawing themselves for a season from the public eye ...

A suspect named John Williams was arrested and charged with these murders. De Quincey describes Williams and the events of Saturday, 7 December:

Williams was a man of middle stature (five feet seven-and-a-half to five feet eight inches high), slenderly built, rather thin, but wiry, tolerably muscular, and clear of all superfluous flesh. A lady, who saw him under examination, assured me that his hair was of the most extraordinary and vivid colour, viz, bright yellow, something between an orange and a lemon colour. In other respects, his appearance was natural enough; and, judging by a plaster cast of him, which I purchased in London, I should say mean, as regarded his facial structure. One fact, however, was striking, and fell in with the impression of his natural tiger character, that his face wore at all times a bloodless ghastly palor ... Into this perilous region [Ratcliffe Highway] it was that, on a Saturday night in December, Mr Williams forced his way through the crowded streets, bound on business ... He carried his tools closely buttoned up under his loose roomy coat ... Marr was the name of that unhappy man who had been selected for the subject of this present Saturday night's performance ... The minutes are numbered and the sands of the hour-glass are running out, that measure the duration of this feud on earth. This night it shall cease. Tomorrow is the day which in England they call Sunday, which in Scotland they call by the Judaic name of 'Sabbath'. The night was one of exceeding darkness; and in this humble quarter of London, whatever the night happened to be, light or dark, quiet or stormy, all shops were kept open on Saturday nights until twelve o'clock, at the least, and many for half an hour longer ... Marr's position in life was this: he kept a little hosier's shop, and had invested in his stock, and the fittings of his shop, about £180. Like all men engaged in trade, he suffered some anxieties. He was a new beginner; but, already, bad debts had alarmed him; and bills were coming to maturity that were not likely to be met by commensurate sales. At this time he was a stout, fresh-coloured young man of twenty-seven.

The household of Marr, consisting of five persons, is as follows: First, there is himself, who if he should happen to be ruined, in a limited commercial sense, has energy enough to jump up again, like a pyramid of fire, and soar high above ruin many times repeated. Yes, poor Marr, so it might be, if thou wert left to thy native energies unmolested; but even now there stands on the other side of the street one born of hell, who puts his peremptory negative on all these flattering prospects. Second in the list of this household, stands his pretty and amiable wife, who is happy after the fashion of youthful wives, for she is only twenty-two, and anxious (if at all) only on account of her darling infant. For, thirdly, there is in a cradle, not quite nine feet below the street viz., in a warm cosy kitchen, and rocked at intervals by the young mother, a baby eight months old. Nineteen months have Marr and herself been married; and this is their first-born child. Grieve not for this child, that it must keep the deep rest of Sunday in some other world; for wherefore should an orphan steeped to the lips in poverty, when once bereaved of father and mother , linger upon an alien and murderous earth? Fourthly, there is a stoutish boy , an apprentice, say thirteen years old; a Devonshire boy, with handsome features, such as most Devonshire youths have; satisfied with his place, not overworked; treated kindly, and aware that he was treated kindly. Fifthly, and lastly, is a servant girl, a grown-up young woman; and she, being particularly kind-hearted, occupies (as often happens in families of humble pretensions as to rank) a sort of sisterly place in her relation to her mistress.

To this young woman it was that suddenly, within three or four minutes of midnight, Marr called aloud from the head of the stairs — directing her to go out and purchase some oysters for the family supper. Upon what slender accidents hang oft-times solemn life-long results! Marr occupied in the concerns of his shop, Mrs Marr occupied with some little ailment and restlessness of her baby, had both forgotten the affair of supper; the time was now; the time was now narrowing every moment, as regarded any variety of choice; and oysters were perhaps ordered as the likeliest article to be had at all, after twelve o'clock should have struck. And yet, upon this trivial circumstance depended Mary's life. It had now become necessary to be quick. Hastily, therefore, receiving from Marr, with a basket in her hand, but unbonneted, Mary tripped out of the shop. It became afterwards, on recollection, a heart-chilling remembrance to herself that, precisely as she emerged from the shop-door, she noticed, on the opposite side of the street, by the light of the lamps, a man's figure; stationary at the instant, but in the next instant slowly moving. This man was Williams…

Williams waited, of necessity, for the sound of a passing watchman's retreating steps; waited, perhaps for thirty seconds; but when the danger was past, the next danger was, lest Marr should lock the door; one turn of the key, and the murderer would have been locked out. In, therefore, he bolted, and by a dextrous movement of his left hand, no doubt, turned the key, without letting Marr perceive this fatal stratagem …

The poor girl roamed up and down in search of an oyster shop; and finding none that was still open, within any circuit that her ordinary experience had made her acquainted with, she fancied it best to try the chances of some remoter district. Lights she saw gleaming or twinkling at a distance, that still tempted her onwards; and thus, amongst unknown streets poorly lighted, and on a night of peculiar darkness, and in a region of London where ferocious tumults were continually turning her out of what seemed to be the direct course, naturally she got bewildered. At length by his lantern she recognised a watchman; through him she was guided into the right road; and in ten minutes more, she found herself back at the door of No. 29 in Ratcliffe Highway …

Mary rang, and at the same time very gently knocked. She had no fear of disturbing her master or mistress; then she made sure of finding them still up. Her anxiety was for the baby, who being disturbed might again rob her mistress of a night's rest. And she well knew that, with three people all anxiously awaiting her return, and by this time, perhaps, seriously uneasy at her delay, the least audible whisper from herself would in a moment bring one of them to the door.

Most naturally at this moment something like hysterical horror over-shadowed the poor girl, and now at last she rang the bell with the violence that belongs to sickening terror. Still as death she was: and during that dreadful stillness, when she hushed her breath that she might listen, occurred an incident of killing fear, that to her dying day would never cease to renew its echoes in her ear. She, Mary, the poor trembling girl, checking and overruling herself by a final effort, that she might leave full opening for her dear young mistress's answer to her own frantic appeal heard at last and most distinctly a sound within the house. On the stairs, not the stairs that led downwards to the kitchen, but the stairs the led upwards to the single storey of bed-chambers above, was heard a creaking sound. Next was heard most distinctly a footfall: one, two, three. Four, five stairs were slowly and distinctly descended. Then the dreadful footsteps were heard advancing along the little narrow passage to the door. The steps- oh heavens! Whose steps? – have paused at the door. The very breathing can be heard of that dreadful being, who has silenced all breathing except his own in the house. There is but a door between him and Mary. What is he doing on the other side of the door? A cautious step, a stealthy step it was that came down the stairs, then paced along the little narrow passage – narrow as a coffin- till at last the step pauses at the door. How hard the fellow breathes! He the solitary murderer, is on one side of the door; Mary is on the other side. Now suppose that he should suddenly open the door, and that incautiously in the dark Mary should rush in, and find herself in the arms of the murderer … The unknown murderer and she have both their lips upon the door, listening, breathing hard; but luckily they are on different sides of the door; and upon the least indication of unlocking, or unlatching, she would have recoiled into the asylum of general darkness.

Mary began now to ring the bell and to ply the knocker with unintermitting violence. And the natural consequence was, that the next door neighbour, who had recently gone to bed and instantly fallen asleep, was roused.

The poor girl remained sufficiently mistress of herself rapidly to explain the circumstance of her own absence for an hour; her belief that Mr and Mrs Marr's family had all been murdered in the interval and that at this very moment the murderer was in the house.

The person to whom she addressed this statement was a pawnbroker; and a thoroughly brave man he must have been; for it was a perilous undertaking, merely as a trial of physical strength, singly to face a mysterious assassin. A brock wall, 9 or 10 feet high, divided his own back premises from those of Marr. Over this he vaulted; and at the moment when he was recalling himself to the necessity of going back for a candle, he suddenly perceived a feeble ray of light already glimmering on some part of Marr's premises. Marr's back door stood wide open. Probably the murderer had passed through it one half minute before. Rapidly the brave man passed onwards to the shop, and there beheld the carnage of the night stretched out on the floor, and the narrow premises so floated with gore, that it was hardly possible to escape the pollution of blood in picking out a path to the front door.

By this time the heart-shaking news involved in the outcries of Mary had availed, even at that late hour, to gather a small mob about the house. The pawnbroker threw open the door. One or two watchmen headed the crowd; but the soul-harrowing spectacle checked them, and impressed sudden silence upon their voices, previously so loud. The tragic drama read aloud its own history ...

Suddenly some person appeared amongst the crowd who was aware that the murdered parents had a young infant; this would be found either below stairs, or in one of the bedrooms above. Immediately a stream of people poured down into the kitchen, where at once they saw the cradle- but with the bedclothes in a state of indescribable confusion. On disentangling these, pools of blood became visible; and the next ominous sign was, that the hood at the head of the cradle had been smashed to pieces. It became evident that the wretch had found himself doubly embarrassed – first, by the arched hood at the head of the cradle, which accordingly he had beat into a ruin with his mallet, and secondly, by the gathering of the blankets and pillows about the baby's head. The free play of his blows had thus been baffled. And he had therefore finished the scene by applying his razor to the throat of the little innocent; after which, with no apparent purpose, as though he had become confused by the spectacle of his own atrocities, he had busied himself in piling the clothes elaborately over the child's corpse.

Following the last spate of murders on 19 December 1811, when a man by the name of Williamson, landlord of the *King's Arms*, 81 New Gravel Lane (now Garnet Street), his wife and an elderly maidservant were similarly murdered, a sailor's maul or hammer was discovered. They were identified as belonging to a labourer named John Williams and this led to his apprehension at the *Pear Tree Tavern* in Cinnamon Street. He was remanded to Coldbath Fields Prison (situated where Mount Pleasant sorting office stands today), pending further investigation. On 28 December, Williams was found hanging from a beam in his cell. Some said he had cheated justice, others took a different view and it was suggested that John Williams was not guilty of the killings and that he did not commit suicide but was himself murdered, to prevent him telling the truth when he came to trial.

On 31 December the remains of John Williams were taken to St George's watch-house, in preparation for his interment. Williams' body was placed on a cart on an inclined platform, so as to afford the public a better view, and the maul and ripping chisel were placed on either side above his head. Escorted by the High Constable of Middlesex and hundreds of constables, officials and parish officers, the procession advanced slowly up Ratcliffe Highway, both followed and watched by immense crowds of people many of whom carried torches. When the cart came opposite the late Mr Marr's house, it halted for nearly a quarter of an hour. It then continued on its journey down Old Gravel Lane, along Wapping Wall, up New Crane Lane before it once again joined Ratcliffe Highway. The cart carrying the body ended its journey at St George's Turnpike at what is now the crossroads at Cable Street and Cannon Street Road, which was where Willams was buried in a grave over which the main water pipe ran, with a stake through his heart. During the hours of darkness, between twelve and one o'clock the body was taken from the platform and lowered into the grave and then a stake was driven through it before the grave was filled in.

This practice of burying suicides at crossroads with a stake through the heart was by no means unusual, as it was common for the

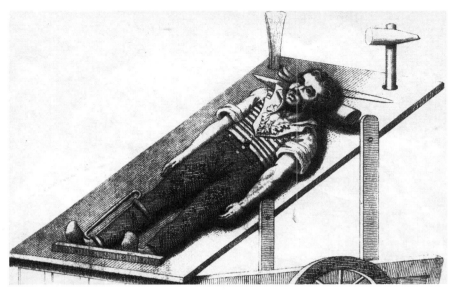

A nineteenth century engraving showing the body of John Williams, placed on an inclined platform, to afford the crowds a better view, as it is drawn through the streets on a cart. The ripping chisel and maul with which he supposedly murdered his victims are displayed above his head. Author's collection

A nineteenth century engraving showing the cart bearing the body of John Williams, having been paraded through the streets, arriving at St George's Turnpike at what is today's junction of Cannon Street Road and Cable Street. Williams was buried there with a stake through his heart and his body covered with quicklime. The grave, deliberately dug too small, can be seen in the right foreground. Author's collection

Church to refuse burial of a suicide victim (or self murderer as some would have it) in consecrated ground. The origins of this practice are vested in pre-empting the vengeance of the suicide's ghost on those who had driven the person to the act. Various acts of indignity were sometimes inflicted on the corpse, such as the cutting off of the right hand to render its ghost less formidable. The theory was that a stake being driven through the heart would prevent the ghost from 'walking'. The additional protection of burying a suicide at a crossroads would be sure to confuse a malevolent spirit about direction. The last such burial took place at the junction of Grosvenor Place and the Kings Road, Chelsea, when a man named Griffiths was buried there in 1823. That same year Parliament passed an Act allowing burials in churchyards, a move instigated by King George IV, who had been delayed by such a burial. The Church continued to take a dim view of suicides and their burials were usually confined to out of the way places or 'suicides corner', interment usually taking place at night between the hours of nine o'clock and midnight, without any form of religious ceremony. In Acts of Parliament passed in 1879 and 1882 suicide ceased to be legally regarded as homicide and burial during daylight hours was

A December 2004 view of the crossroads where John Williams was buried on 31 January 1811. The author

allowed. However, it was not until 1961 that suicide was finally decriminalised.

P D James and T A Critchley in their account of the Ratcliffe Highway murders, wrote in *The Maul and the Pear Tree*,

> *Here a long hole about four feet deep, three feet long and two feet wide, had been dug ready. The hole was too small for the body, deliberately so. There was no intention that these ignoble limbs should lie in the semblance of innocent sleep, or be decently disposed as if laid out for Christian burial. Williams's body was seized, tumbled roughly out of the cart, and forced into the hole. Immediately one of the escorts jumped down beside it and began to drive the stake through the heart. As the blood-stained maul thudded on the stake, the silence of the crowd was at last broken and the air became hideous with shouts and execrations.*

The centuries of notoriety that the name Ratcliffe was associated with, compounded by the murders of 1811, resulted in a gradual edging out of the name. Sadly, today the name Ratcliffe has almost vanished from the East End. The hamlet is no more but its name lives on in Ratcliffe Cross Street.

CHAPTER 4

Henry Wainright and the Murder of Harriet Lane
1874–75

I'll give you £100, I'll give you £200, and produce the money in twenty minutes if you'll let me go.

On the afternoon of Saturday, 11 September 1875 one of the most unusual, if not macabre, chases ever to take place in London, began in the Whitechapel Road. A four-wheeled cab was followed on foot by a perspiring and breathless young brushmaker named Alfred Stokes. When the opportunity allowed, he called out for police assistance from time to time, but this was to no avail. Stokes followed the cab to the Commercial Road, where it stopped briefly near the corner of Greenfield Street to pick up a female passenger. The chase continued through the city as the cab made its way to the river, then across London Bridge, before it ended its journey in High Street, Borough. The cab stopped at the junction with Southwark Street, at a group of buildings known as the Hen and Chickens.

It was there that a man got out of the cab and took from the front seat a parcel, which he carried into the Hen and Chickens. Just as the man had entered the building Alfred Stokes spotted a policeman and spoke to him. Shortly afterwards, as the man came out of the building and went once again to the cab for a second parcel, the policeman approached him and a conversation took place. Another policeman arrived and both constables accompanied the man, who was still carrying his parcel, into the Hen and Chickens. A little while later they emerged from the building and the man and the woman, who remained waiting inside the cab, were taken into custody and driven to Stone's End Police Station. The two parcels were taken to St Saviour's mortuary.

The man taken into custody was Henry Wainwright, former proprietor of a brushmaker's business in the long and broad thoroughfare known as the Whitechapel Road. The young woman was Miss Alice Day, a member of the ballet company at the Pavilion

Theatre, also in the Whitechapel Road. The crudely chopped up pieces of human remains that were the contents of the two parcels, were later identified as the complete body of a woman aged between twenty to twenty-five years. Evidence later produced showed the remains to be those of Harriet Louisa Lane, otherwise known as Mrs Percy King, a woman of about twenty-four years of age.

Henry Wainwright. Author's collection

Henry Wainwright, was a mat and brushmaker, who was in business with his brother William, at 84 and 215 Whitechapel Road. Their father, a respectable tradesman and churchwarden of his parish, had died in 1864, leaving a fortune of £11,000 to be divided between his four sons and a daughter. Henry Wainwright, described as a 'gentleman,' had married in 1862, the daughter of a 'merchant,' In appearance he was described as moderately tall, thick and broad-shouldered in build. He had blue eyes, a large nose and his dark brown hair and beard was waved and curly. His beard and moustache concealed a heavy and sensual mouth. It was said that the whole effect of the face was by no means displeasing, and to women, Henry Wainwright was very attractive. He possessed all the gifts that make a man popular. He was genial, hospitable and always ready to 'stand a treat'. He was intelligent and had a deep interest in intellectual pursuits. He dressed well and, keeping with the fashions of the day, invariably wore a high hat. In 1860, when he was twenty-two, he was a prominent member of the Christ Church Institute, St George's in-the-East, and a particular supporter of its music and elocution classes. Around this time he gave an entertainment in an East-End school, described as *An Evening with Thomas More*. He also took an active part in amateur theatricals. He appeared in the part of Tom Cranky in *The Birthplace of Podgers,* the part made famous by the noted Victorian actor J L Toole. He also gave occasional readings of the works of Charles Dickens and Thomas Hood amongst others. In 1867, Wainwright delivered a lecture at the Leeds Mechanics' Institution on *The Wit and Eccentricity of Sydney Smith*. He also featured as a temperance lecturer but he was not long in abandoning those principles.

Wainwright's shop was situated on the north side of Whitechapel Road, at 84, and almost opposite, on the south side, was his warehouse at 215. Vine Court, which ran from Whitechapel Road, along one side of the *Royal Oak,* allowed access to the rear of Wainwright's warehouse, and was an ideal means of entering or leaving his premises unnoticed. The Pavilion Theatre stood immediately next door to his shop, near the junction of Baker's Row (today's Vallance Road). Wainwright supplied the theatre with mats and brushes, he was on good terms with the management, and he was always a welcome and highly regarded patron, as he showed great interest in all things connected with the activities there, and enjoyed practically the free run of the theatre. He

Plan of Whitechapel Road as it was during Henry Wainwright's occupancy of No.'s 84 and 135. Author's collection

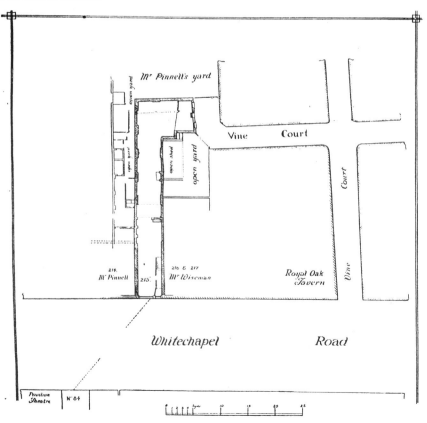

was often there both as a member of the audience and as a back stage visitor to the actors, dancers and other members of the company. He was always lavish in entertaining, and to the actors getting very humble salaries, it was considered a much-deserved privilege to be asked out to sup with Mr Wainwright. Of Wainwright himself, it was said that vanity played no part in his character.

In 1871, thirty-three years-old Henry Wainwright, was living with his wife and family in Chingford, Essex. During that year he had a chance meeting with a young lady of about twenty years of age, on the banks of the River Lea, at the popular pleasure resort known as Broxbourne Gardens. This meeting was to have unfortunate and fatal consequences for both parties concerned. The young lady, Harriet Louisa Lane, was the daughter of John Lane, a gas manager employed in the Royal Gunpowder Mills at Waltham Abbey. Wainwright was at that time one of the most respected businessmen in the Whitechapel Road. Harriet Lane lived at Waltham Cross and was apprenticed to a milliner and dressmaker at Waltham Abbey. She was described as a golden haired, lively little woman, with pleasing manners and a love of finery. Henry Wainwright and Harriet Lane were attracted to each other and they began an affair. It appears that Harriet was aware, early in the relationship, that Wainwright was a married man with a family.

Letters, in Henry Wainwright's hand, found among Harriet Lane's belongings and written in the years 1871 and 1872 indicate that their intimate, clandestine relationship was commenced under assumed names. Wainwright passing himself off as 'George Williams,' and Harriet Lane as 'Miss L. Varco'. In July 1871, Williams writes:

Darling creature, off to Paris – for God's sake don't write, etc. Drop me a line in about a fortnight (if you don't in that time thoroughly forget me) to P.O., Whitechapel Road. Oceans of Love.

On 25 August he made an appointment to meet Miss Varco in the first-class waiting room at Bishopsgate Station, and in September he wrote to her from Germany, this time signing himself George Varco:

It is very uncertain how long I shall stay away from England, perhaps for ever, God knows, so think no more of me, and quite forget you ever saw me. I have told P.O. to send me only letters received in name of
Yrs most affectionately
Geo. Varco

A letter from Strasbourg follows this:

My little Beauty, not home till December, drop me a line to P.O. by Dec. 1st, if you don't forget me, as in all probability you will.

40 Tredegar Square, Bow, onetime home to the Wainwright family, seen here in December 2004. No. 40 is the door to the right of the centre pediment. Apart from the tarmac road and an abundance of motor vehicles, Tredegar Square is substantially the same, in appearance, as it was during the Wainwright family's occupancy. The author

In February 1872 there appeared in the *Waltham Abbey and Cheshunt Weekly Telegraph* an advertisement. It stated that on the 22nd instant, at St Mary's, Percy King Esq, of Chelsea, had been married to Harriet, ninth daughter of John Lane, of Waltham Cross, Herts. Unbeknown to his wife, family and friends, Wainwright set up home with Harriet at 14, St Peter Street (now Cephas Street), Mile End, and they lived together as Mr and Mrs Percy King. Wainwright gave Harriet £5 a week, a considerable sum of money in those days. It was at 14, St Peter Street that a daughter was born on 22 August 1872. Wainwright successfully managed to lead this double life but when he moved from Chingford to 40 Tredegar Square, Bow, perhaps he thought the proximity of his mistress to his wife and family was too much of a risk and he moved Harriet to the West End, firstly to Alfred Street, Bedford Square and later to Cecil Street, Strand.

A pleasant account of the home life of Wainwright at this time, and an instance of his natural friendliness and geniality are given by J B Howe, an East-End tragedian of the day, in his book *A Cosmopolitan Actor*:

A few days after my arrival, I left my house in Tredegar Terrace, Bow, to proceed westward, and as I crossed Tredegar Square I saw a hansom cab drawing up to the centre house of the row. A gentleman of medium height jumped out, and approaching me exclaimed "Bless me, I can't be mistaken. It's Mr Howe." "You have the advantage of me," I replied, and yet your face is familiar!" "Oh yes, I've seen you often at the East London; come into the house if you have a moment to spare, I can give you a glass of sherry."

After having addressed the cabman and rung the bell, the door was opened by a smart slavey, and he led the way to an elegantly furnished parlour. Wine was brought on the table, with biscuits, and while we were chatting about my travels, the door was gently opened and a pretty, dark lady entered with two lovely children. The gentleman merely said: "My wife, Mr Howe."

The lady took a seat and seemed greatly pleased with the interest her husband evinced in the hurried explanation I gave of my voyage home, and, amongst other remarks, I elicited from him the fact that he was in some sense an actor himself. "That is," said he, "I play for charitable purposes sometimes, and also give lectures at the Bow and Bromley Institute and other places."

All this time I did not like to put the somewhat rude question, "What might be your name?" thinking, of course, that he would divulge it in the course of the glib conversation; but, however, he did not, and after a lapse of perhaps thirty-five minutes, he left the room to make some explanations to his wife, and re-entering exclaimed –

"Were you going to the city?"

"I was going to the West End when I encountered you."

"Oh then, you can come in my cab as far as Whitechapel, if you have no objection."

"None in the least," I rejoined.

"All right jump in; good-bye my dears." Then kissing the children and his wife he joined me, and we turned into the Bow Road towards Mile End. As we drove along, I thought I had never in my life encountered a nicer man. A fine head, firmly balanced on square shoulders; raven locks, and large penetrating blue eyes, short whiskers just tinged with a red sandy hue, and a power of conversation really wonderful. He asked me where I intended to open in London. I told him I really did not know, as I had not yet shown myself. By this time we were at Mile End. "Well," he exclaimed, "as I am so near my shop, I'll just jump out and leave you."

He alighted, shook hands with a friend, and walked away arm in arm towards the London Hospital.

"Who was that gentleman?" I asked the cabman, "I did not like to ask him his name, he seemed to know me well enough." "You must have seen him often" said the cabman. "Its Henry Wainwright, the brushmaker."

Wainwright clearly had a change of heart about lodging Harriet in the West End because by late 1873, she was once again living at St Peter Street, this time at No 70, where she gave birth to a second daughter on 3 December. Perhaps there were financial considerations in moving Harriet back to St Peter Street. In May 1874 Harriet went to lodge with Mrs Foster, who lived in Sidney Street, off Sidney Square, very close to Wainwright's business premises.

For three years Henry Wainwright had been leading this double life. It is not known for certain how many people knew of his relationship with Harriet, but it must have been only a few who had been brought into close contact with 'Mrs King'. Among these was Miss Ellen Wilmore, for whom Harriet had worked at one time as a dressmaker. It appears that Miss Wilmore was fond of Harriet, and, when she learnt of her connection with 'Mr King', had with Wainwright's approval, taken care of the elder of the little girls. However, beyond Miss Wilmore, few if any knew the true identity of

Mr Percy King. Had Wainwright's business continued to prosper he would have had no difficulty in fulfilling his responsibilities towards his clandestine family, so rendering the possibility of the exposure of his misconduct unlikely. Unfortunately, Henry Wainwright's fortunes took a turn for the worse.

Wainwright's business affairs had been going steadily from bad to worse, possibly through his own neglect and extravagance. It was generally believed that Wainwright conducted other clandestine affairs, which would have been a further drain on his finances. By the beginning of 1874 his financial affairs reached a crisis. His brother William, to whom he owed a considerable sum of money, dissolved their partnership. An attempt by Wainwright to carry on the business with a new partner, Mr Sawyer, ended disastrously. His debts, not including the money owed to his brother, amounted to over £3,000. In May his creditors met and agreed to accept a composition of 12 shillings in the pound, of which, however, Wainwright, due to escalating events, never paid more than 9 shillings In July he was so hard up for cash that he found it necessary to pawn a revolver.

These financial embarrassments had put an unwelcome strain on the relationship between Wainwright and 'Mrs King'. The £5 that she had been receiving at the beginning of their relationship had dwindled and it reached the point that it was only with considerable difficulty that she was able to extract any money from him at all. Far from being kept like a lady, as she had been used to, as Wainwright's financial problems increased, he considered Harriet and her family little more than an irksome encumbrance. However, Mr and Mrs King's two little girls were being looked after by Miss Wilmore, who received money for their maintenance from Wainwright. Harriet was obliged to pawn several of her personal items and the pressure she was under induced her to take more strong drink than was good for her. Often under the influence of drink, she would turn up at Wainwright's shop at 84 Whitechapel Road and make a scene. Sometime during the summer of 1874, when in a drunken state, Harriet created a scene outside her lodgings in Sidney Street, she was given notice to quit by her landlady.

At the beginning of September 1874, Henry Wainwright took out a mortgage on his warehouse premises at 215 Whitechapel Road. Owing to his mistress's inconvenient devotion to him, he could see no prospect of palming her off on another man. Her now only too frequent appearances at his shop and the unpleasant scenes she created, were becoming not only an embarrassment but risked the

Whitechapel Road, seen here in December 2004. What remains of Henry Wainwright's warehouse, in 1875 No 215, is occupied by 'Fix-A-Phone', now No. 136. The building that was once the **Royal Oak** *is now a shop, six buildings further down the street.* The author

possibility of his exposure. Clearly he felt the continuance of his relationship with Harriet Lane, far too great a risk to take. On 10 September he ordered half a hundred weight of chloride of lime which was packed in a box and sent to his shop. At four o'clock the following afternoon, Friday 11 September, Mrs Percy King left her lodgings. The living space above Wainwright's warehouse was vacant and she had designs on staying there. She mentioned this to her friend, Miss Wilmore. She was carrying a small parcel which contained a nightdress. She told Miss Wilmore, that she was going to meet 'enry Wainwright at his place in the Whitechapel Road' No one ever reported having seen her alive again.

Three men working next door to Wainwright's warehouse swore that, on an evening about this time in September, between half-past

A present-day view of Henry Wainwright's warehouse. The rear portion of the building shown on the plan, which included the 'paint shop', has been demolished many years ago.
The author

five and six o'clock they heard three pistol shots fired in rapid succession, which appeared to come from the direction of Wainwright's premises. The warehouse at 215 Whitechapel Road was a long, narrow building, some forty yards in depth. A good deal of the flooring was stone, but at the extreme end was a raised portion, called the paint room, the floor of which was of wood. It was beneath the floor of the paint room that Henry Wainwright buried the body of his mistress in chloride of lime. Harriet Lane had been shot through the head and her lover had also cut her throat . Wainwright clearly believed that the chloride of lime would quickly dissolve the soft tissue of Harriet's body and soon there would be virtually no remains to link him with her murder. How wrong he was.

Naturally, Harriet's disappearance had to be explained. Wainwright told Miss Wilmore and those of Harriet's relations who inquired as to her whereabouts, that she had gone off with a man named Teddy Frieake, with whom she was living on the continent. In fact Miss Wilmore received a letter purporting to come from Mr Frieake, addressed from the *Charing Cross Hotel*, in which the writer said that Mrs King had promised to have no more to do with Mr King or her family and friends. On these conditions Mr Frieake was going to marry her, and they were about to start for Dover. On 17 October both Henry Wainwright and Miss Wilmore received telegrams from Frieake sent from Dover, saying that he and Harriet were off to the Continent for a spree.

Wainwright made a foolish mistake when he chose to use the name Teddy Frieake. Not only was the surname unusual in itself but that particular spelling was extremely uncommon. In doing so he risked his affair to Harriet Lane being more widely exposed, because of the attention Frieake's name attracted, as well as casting doubt on her having gone away with Teddy Frieake in the first place. According to Wainwright, this Edward or 'Teddy' Frieake was a friend of his, and on several occasions during 1873 and the early part of 1874, Wainwright and a person calling himself Edward Frieake had visited Harriet at her lodgings. Her landlady confirmed this. It appears that this visitor calling himself Edward Frieake was none other than Henry Wainwright's brother, Thomas, as the letter written from the *Charing Cross Hotel*, supposedly sent by Frieake, was in Thomas Wainwright's hand. Henry Wainwright had a friend or at least an acquaintance by the name of Edward Frieake, an auctioneer and public house valuer, with offices at 11 Coleman Street, City and auction rooms at 14 & 15 Aldgate. He lived in Bow and had known Wainwright for over fourteen years. The real Edward Frieake said 'I was on terms of intimacy with him for many years; he used to address me as 'Teddy' or 'Frieaky,' and I used to address him as 'Harry.' I have lived at Bow for nearly sixteen years. Up to September last I was on friendly terms with him.'

Towards the end of August 1874 Edward Frieake received a letter at his Coleman Street offices; he said, 'I read it of course, but I did not know the writer. I never knew a person named L. King to my knowledge. I was utterly astonished and could not imagine what it referred to.' It seems that Wainwright was trying to convince Harriet that Teddy Frieake was in love with her. It has been suggested that his intention might have been to get his brother to take her away and leave her in some far away place with no means of returning home. Instead, Henry Wainwright resorted to more drastic measures to dispose of his encumbrance.

Somehow Harriet Lane had obtained the real Teddy Frieake's address and written to him. Once those concerned with the whereabouts of Harriet Lane had made contact with the real Teddy Frieake and they had showed him the letter sent from the *Charing Cross Hotel* matters became very confused and rather unpleasant. He produced the letter sent to him by L King and after some discussion with Harriet's relations Edward Frieake paid a visit to Henry Wainwright at his shop. Wainwright tried to assure Mr Frieake that the Teddy Frieake concerned was another man entirely, a music-hall performer. Mr Frieake was not convinced that some sort of chicanery was not afoot and Frieake fell out with Wainwright. In November 1874, Thomas Wainwright, who had impersonated Teddy Frieake, started an ironmongery business at the Hen and Chickens, Borough.

The actor Frank Tyars, for many years a member of Henry Irving's company, was engaged at the Pavilion Theatre at different times during 1874 and 1875. He described Henry Wainwright as he first knew him, as a man of a very self-assured and confident bearing, who walked down the Whitechapel Road as if it belonged to him, hail-fellow-well-met in his manner, cordial and friendly towards all those associated with the theatre. Before the summer of 1874 Tyars left the Pavilion, but returned there later to fulfil another engagement. It was then that he noticed an extraordinary change in the demeanour of Wainwright. He first saw him coming down the street. Instead of the breezy, self-confident gentleman he had known, he saw a man walking slowly along in a furtive, hang-dog way, and, to his astonishment, recognised him as Henry Wainwright.

J B Howe had also observed a change in the man. He had become nervous, impatient and irritable. He had taken to visiting public-houses, where he would sit drinking more than was good for him, and nervously cracking and eating walnuts, of which he was very fond.

Fortunately for Wainwright, those who knew him, including the popular tragedian, put down this marked change in his manner and disposition to his business and financial difficulties. On 27 November 1874, Wainwright's shop at 84 Whitechapel Road was burnt down, its contents completely gutted by the fire. He claimed £3,000 insurance money from the Sun Fire Office, but the company

The building that until fairly recently was occupied by the Royal Oak. *The name of the pub can still be seen above the second-floor windows. The entrance to Vine Court can be seen on the right.* The author

disputed his claim. He brought an action against them, which had not yet come on for trial at the time of his arrest. Wainwright was in the habit of speaking with great excitement and bitterness of the conduct of the Sun Fire Office in resisting his claim. On one such occasion J B Howe found himself very nearly involved in a row in the bar of the *Royal Oak* owing to some expression he had used in trying to calm Wainwright's too outspoken indignation against his insurers.

On 30 June 1875, Henry Wainwright was declared bankrupt. In July the mortgagee of 215 Whitechapel Road foreclosed and took possession of the premises, including that portion known as the 'paint room' under which lay the remains of Harriet Lane. By this time Wainwright had given up working for himself. He had taken employment as a manager from Mr Martin, a well-to-do corn merchant in the New Road, Whitechapel. Mr Martin had taken over Wainwright's brushmaking business in an amicable way, and advanced him £300. He paid Wainwright a salary of £3 a week, and intended when the money he had advanced him had been paid off to restore him to his business. Wainwright was in the habit of calling at 215 for his letters, and would seem to have had access to the premises. Many persons had noticed, at different times, an unpleasant smell in the warehouse, and an inquisitive dog that nosed about too frequently in the neighbourhood was said to have disappeared suddenly.

The ironmongery business set up by Thomas Wainwright in November 1874, failed. In June 1875 Thomas' principal creditor put in an execution and a sale was held on the 28 of that month. After the sale the premises were locked up but Thomas Wainwright retained the key. The foundations of the buildings known as the Hen and Chickens were deep and solid, and down in its cellars were some remote and inaccessible corners, convenient hiding places for inconvenient relics.

Henry Wainwright must have come to the conclusion that 215 Whitechapel Road was no longer a safe depository for Harriet Lane's remains and he decided to remove them. Doubts were long entertained about Thomas Wainwright's involvement in the murder of Harriet Lane but in *The Chronicles of Newgate* by Arthur Griffiths, published in 1883, he states 'a conversation overheard between the two brothers in Newgate satisfactorily exonerated Thomas Wainwright.' Exactly when Thomas became aware of what had become of his brother's mistress is not known. Clearly he knew something by at least as early as 10 September 1875, but it is possible that he knew long before then. Henry Wainwright and possibly Thomas must have lifted the floorboards either on the morning of 10 September or sometime previously, and discovered that instead of destroying the body, as was the intention, the chloride of lime had in fact preserved it. Despite its relatively good state of preservation, the remains were, nevertheless, a stinking mess.

On 10 September Henry and Thomas Wainwright purchased between them, some American cloth, some rope, a spade and chopper. The spade and chopper were purchased from Frederick Pettigrew, an ironmonger trading at 81 Whitechapel Road, by Thomas Wainwright at between twelve and one o'clock. Mr Pettigrew said at the trial 'I charged him 3*s*. for the two, because he was in the trade. The retail price was 5*s*. It would be impossible for me to say if the spade and axe produced are the same, because I supply other ironmongers with the same sort of articles.'

The work of removing Harriet Lane's remains from beneath the floorboards of the paint room was probably carried out sometime on 10 September. The body was crudely chopped up and the various body parts were made into two separate parcels wrapped up in the American cloth and tied with rope. Next morning, Saturday 11 September, exactly a year after Harriet Lane had left her lodgings in Sidney Street, a friend of Thomas Wainwright remarked he was not looking well.

About four o'clock that afternoon Henry Wainwright asked Alfred Stokes, who lived nearby at 34 Bakers' Row (today's Vallance Road) if he would help him carry some parcels from his old warehouse. Stokes, although still a young man, had known Henry Wainwright for seventeen or eighteen years and had for most of that time been in his employ as an out-worker. More recently he had become Wainwright's fellow manager in the employ of Mr Martin. He was more than happy to oblige his highly regarded, former employer, Mr Wainwright. He accompanied him to No 215. Stokes said at the trial:

I knew the premises No. 215 Whitechapel Road as a packing place. West, his chief clerk, who lived there first, left sometime in July, 1874, and from that time no one lived there until Mr Rogers went to occupy them in November of the same year. They were shut up at night, but were used for packing purposes. I believe the keys were always left in the counting-house at No. 84 until the fire. Henry Wainwright went out of business about a month before he went into Mr Martin's service. He told me he was living at Schoolhouse Lane, Chingford, but I never went there. In September of this year, on Thursday or Friday, the 9th or 10th, I believe, but I cannot say which, I had some conversation with Henry. I told him I had bought a chain for the scales. He said, "Oh yes! It is very useful, and then he said, "I have a chopper and a shovel to sell likewise which will be very useful." I said, "Yes, so they will, sir, as we require them for the place." I next saw him on the Saturday morning, but nothing happened till about half-past four, when in Mr Martin's presence, he said, "Will you carry a parcel for me, Stokes?" I said, "Yes sir, with the greatest of pleasure." We then went together to 215 Whitechapel Road, in through Vine Court to the back of the premises. Henry took a key out of his pocket and opened the door. We both went in, and he told me to go upstairs and fetch down a parcel. I went upstairs, and through by the skylight into the dwelling-room, 80 or 90 feet from the point where we came in, but did not find the parcel. I came downstairs and told him I could not find it; he said, "Never mind Stokes, I will find them where I placed them a fortnight ago, under the straw." I saw some straw up in a corner, and two parcels wrapped in black American cloth, and tied up with rope. He said, "These are the parcels I want you to carry Stokes." I lifted them up and I says, "They are too heavy for me," and put them down. He said, "Wait a bit, Stokes. Here is the shovel and chopper I want you to sell for me." He had told me that he wanted me to sell them to Mr Martin, my employer. I saw a shovel and chopper and a hammer lying near. I said "All right, sir," and I picked up the chopper, and said, "What's this on it? It stinks." I saw some mess on it. He said, "It is only cat's or dog's dirt." He took it in his hands, and wiped it off, and then wiped it on a piece of newspaper, and laid it on the floor ... He afterwards said, "Come along Stokes." I picked up both parcels and followed him. I then said, "I can't carry them; they stink so bad, and the weight of them is too heavy for me." He said, "I will take one off you at the bottom of Vine Court." ... I carried the two parcels out of the premises from Vine Court into Whitechapel Road. He took the lightest of the parcels from me, and we walked to Whitechapel Church, which would be about a quarter of a mile. As we were going on I said "I shall have to rest, sir. It's too heavy for me. I cannot carry it." He replied, "For God's sake don't drop it, or else you will break it."

On arriving at Whitechapel Church, Wainwright told Stokes to mind the parcels while he went to get a cab at a cab-rank a little way off. Stokes was by this time suspicious of the two parcels. They smelt offensively and he believed that Wainwright might be attempting to surreptitiously remove a large quantity of human hair, used by brushmakers and already sold to Mr Martin as part of Wainwright's stock when he purchased the business. Later Stokes said that a supernatural voice had called to him distinctly three times saying, 'Open that parcel.' Whatever his reason, Stokes' curiosity got the better of him and he opened the parcel only to discover, much to his horror, a human hand. Stokes re-tied the parcel and when Wainwright returned after about five minutes, in a four-wheeler, driven by cabman William Andrews of Pearl Street, Spitalfields, he said nothing to him about his discovery. Stokes helped Wainwright put the parcels on the front seat of the cab, and Wainwright told Stokes that he would see him at seven o'clock in the evening. Wainwright then got in and it drove down Church Lane off in the direction of East India Dock then turned round to the left into Commercial Road.

Stokes said that the voice spoke to him again and told him to 'Follow that cab!' Stokes did follow the cab on foot but not without difficulty; he didn't want to be seen by Wainwright. The cab stopped briefly in the Commercial Road, near the junction of Greenfield Street. Henry Wainwright had spotted a lady of his acquaintance. Meanwhile, Alfred Stokes concealed himself in a doorway. Miss Alice Day lived at 8 Queens Court, Greenfield Street. She worked behind the scenes as a seamstress in the ballet at the Pavilion Theatre. Wainwright got out of the cab smoking a large cigar. He asked Alice if she would like to go for a ride with him as far as London Bridge. She said she would as long as she was back by

The Pavilion Theatre, Whitechapel Road, situated next door to Henry Wainwright's shop (not featured, but it stood to the left of the Pavilion Refreshment Room, until destroyed by fire on 27 November 1874). The relatively modest frontage concealed a very large and sumptuous auditorium. This theatre, a favourite haunt of Wainwright, could seat 3,500 patrons and had an enormous stage measuring 70 feet by 58 feet. The theatre's size and varied programme gave it the cachet, the 'Drury Lane of the East End.' Drawn by the author

a quarter-past-six in time to go to the theatre. She got into the cab with Wainwright, who told the cabman to 'Drive on as fast as you can over London Bridge to the Borough' and the cab turned round and drove off in the direction of the city. Wainwright continued to puff on his cigar, which no doubt helped to disguise the stench coming from the parcels. He asked Alice not to speak to him as he needed to think. The cab continued along its journey, Stokes desperately trying to keep up with it, while at the same time attempting to summon help. He ran after the cab until he saw two constables in Leadenhall Street. He said 'I was very exhausted and called their attention to the cab.

The site of the Pavilion Theatre, Whitechapel Road, in December 2004. The frontage occupied the entire space behind the advertising board. The Academy Drama School (incorporating the Andrew Sketchley Theatre) stands on the site once occupied by Wainwright's shop, then No. 84, now No. 189. The author

But they laughed and said, "Man, you must be mad." The cab was then 30 yards at least ahead of me.' He followed it along Leadenhall Street, Fenchurch Street and across London Bridge. He said 'I stopped beside the factory, on the right-hand side of the Borough, which is part of the premises of the London Joint Stock Bank. From the place where it stopped [the building], by standing a little on one side, one can see the Hen and Chickens.'

The cab pulled up in Borough High Street at the junction of Southwark Street and Henry Wainwright got out and carried a parcel into the Hen and Chickens. Alice Day waited in the cab. Alfred Stokes saw a policeman and told him what he had seen in the parcel. The policeman approached the cab and, as he was waiting there,

Wainwright returned. He had already taken the second parcel out of the cab when the police constable, Arthur Cox (policeman M290) approached him. The following conversation took place:

P C Do you live here?
H W No.
P C Have you got possession of this place?
H W I have, and you haven't.
P C Well, go inside.
H W No, perhaps you had better go in.
P C I want to see what's in that parcel you have just taken in.
H W Ask no questions and there's £50 each for you.

This offer of £50 each came because, by this time, another constable had come up (Henry Turner, policeman, M48). The constables said they did not want Wainwright's money, and took him along with them into the Hen and Chickens. There they opened the parcels and found the remains of a human body. Wainwright said desperately 'I'll give you £100, I'll give you £200, and produce the money in twenty minutes if you'll let me go.' But it was all to no avail. The game was up. Both Henry Wainwright and Alice Day were taken into custody and the remains were later removed to the nearby St Saviour's mortuary.

On Monday, 13 September Henry Wainwright, aged thirty-six, described as 'manager of a school' at Chingford, Essex, and Alice Day, aged twenty, dressmaker, were charged at Southwark Police Court with having in their possession the mutilated body of a woman unknown, supposed to have been murdered. At the time of his arrest, Wainwright's family had left Tredegar Square, and were living at School House Lane, Chingford. At this first court hearing the evidence of both Stokes and the constable was taken. Wainwright asked no questions but Alice Day clutched hold of him and said 'For God's sake tell them what I know of the matter – I know nothing.' Both prisoners were remanded. On Wednesday, 15 September an inquest was opened at the Vestry, St Saviours, Southwark. Harriet Lane's father was called as a witness to give evidence as to the identity of the remains. He said they were those of his daughter, but could give no very specific reason for saying so. The body was so far decomposed as to make any recognition of the features out of the question. However, he suddenly remembered that Harriet had been burned on the leg as a child, and that the scar of the burn had remained. The body having then been re-examined it was discovered that there was a distinct scar below the right knee about the size of a two-shilling piece.

On Tuesday, 21 September Henry Wainwright was charged with the wilful murder of Harriet Lane. At the inquest it became perfectly clear that Alice Day knew nothing whatsoever about the murder and she was discharged. On Friday, 1 October, Thomas Wainwright was arrested and on 3 October he was charged at Southwark Police Court with being an accessory after the fact.

In *The Times* report of the last two days' proceedings at Southwark Police Court, the name of W S Gilbert is given as being instructed with Mr Besley for the defence of the prisoner Henry Wainwright. This W S Gilbert was the famous humorist and dramatist,

A memorial to Sir W(illiam) S(chwenck) Gilbert (1836–1911) on the Thames Embankment, Gilbert's name appears as counsel for the defence, in the Police Court proceedings. The author

collaborator with Arthur Sullivan in the Savoy Operas. Though a barrister, Gilbert had at this time given up practice and devoted himself to writing. Much to his annoyance, he found himself summoned to a jury, which might take him away from his writing for an inconvenient time. However, practising barristers were exempted from jury duty. In order to claim his exemption he persuaded a friend to give him a nominal brief for two days in the Wainwright case. As a result his name appears as counsel for the defence in the reports of the proceedings at the Police Court.

Gilbert told H B Irving (the distinguished barrister and son of the great actor Sir Henry Irving) who commented on many great trials of the day, including that of The Wainwrights, a peculiar story regarding his connection with the case. In his later years Henry Wainwright had developed a strong resemblance to the dramatist Tom Robertson, the author of *Caste* and other well known comedies of the day. Robertson died in 1871, the same year Wainwright had met Harriet Lane. Gilbert attended the funeral, and noticed among those standing at the graveside a man who bore a strong resemblance to the deceased dramatist. A little while later Gilbert got into a carriage on the underground railway, and sitting in the corner of the carriage was this same man. The resemblance was so striking that for a moment Gilbert forgot that his friend was dead and was almost at the point of speaking to the stranger. When Gilbert attended at Southwark Police Court and Henry Wainwright came into the dock, Gilbert recognised him at once as the man who had surprised him by his striking resemblance to Tom Robertson.

On Wednesday, 13 October Henry and Thomas Wainwright were committed for trial. The following day, the coroner's jury returned a verdict of wilful murder against Henry Wainwright. The trial of the Wainrights was postponed until the November session. It opened on Monday, 22 November at the Old Bailey and the judge was the Lord Chief Justice of England (Sir James Alexander Cockburn, Bart). The Counsel for the Crown was led by the Attorney General (Sir John Holker, Q C), Mr H B Poland, Mr Beasley and instructed by Mr Pollard on behalf of the Treasury. Counsel for Henry Wainwright were Mr Edward Besley, Mr Douglas Straight, Mr Tickell, Mr C F Gill, instructed by Mr Pelham. The Counsel for Thomas George Wainwright was Mr Moody.

At the trial the whole story of Wainwright's connection with Harriet Lane became clear, as did his brother Thomas' part in the affair, to the satisfaction of the jury. The medical evidence left no doubt as to what had become of Wainwright's mistress. Following the discovery of the remains of Harriet Lane on Saturday, 11 September, they were examined by Frederick George Larkin, surgeon, of No 44 Trinity Square. In his evidence at the trial he said:

> *I was called to see the remains of a human body before half-past five on the afternoon of 11th September. I was shown two parcels containing the remains of a female human body. I then made a short examination, and on the Monday gave some evidence. Some portions of the body were mummified.*
>
> *... Some parts were moist and decomposed, in a state known as adipocere. The parts had been separated very unscientifically. The body had been divided into ten parts – head and neck one part, two hands, two arms, one trunk, two thighs and two legs and feet connected... there were fragments of the pelvis attached to the thighs, and a portion of the kneecap was connected with the left leg. Upon the hair was dried blood. The body had been recently divided.*

Three bullets were found in Harriet's skull during the examination, two having entered the skull itself, the third having been flattened by a velvet covered hair pad, which contained an immense number of hairpins.

Mr Larkin also commented:

> *... Having discovered the bullets, we turned our attention to her cut throat. It was a cut from right to left, beginning just beyond the medial line on the right side of the middle of the neck, across to a point above opposite the angle of the lower jaw on the left side. It had severed all the structures from the windpipe down to the vertebrae. It extended about 2 inches to the left, upwards and backwards, below and opposite the angle of the lower jaw – it must have severed the carotid artery. That cut must have been made immediately before or immediately after death.*

Mr Larkin concluded that he could only give a rough idea of how long the woman had been dead commenting 'I should say from nine to twelve months.'

The remains were also examined by Mr Thomas Bond, surgeon, of 50 Parliament Street, Westminster, assistant surgeon to the Westminster Hospital, and Lecturer on Forensic Medicine at that hospital. He said:

On 16th September last I saw the remains of the body at the dead house. Mr Larkin was present. The body was that of a female of short stature, about 5 feet in height, of slender make, limbs and body. I thought she was from twenty to twenty-five years of age, and that the body had been dead many months. The hands were slender and covered with a greasy substance. The skin underneath was dry and sunken. The feet were in the same condition …

Having carefully considered all the evidence the jury found both prisoners guilty as charged. However, Henry Wainwright did not agree with their verdict. The judge addressed him:

Lord Chief Justice *– I cannot allow you to make a speech. You can only reply to the question whether you have anything to say why sentence should not be passed.*

Henry Wainwright *– Then I will only say, standing as I do now upon the brink of eternity and in the presence of the God before whom I shall shortly appear, that I swear that I am not the murderer of the remains found in my possession. I swear that I have not buried these remains, and the proof that I did not exhume those mutilated remains has been proved before you by witnesses. I have been guilty of great immorality; I have been guilty of many indiscretions; but for the crime of which I have been brought in guilty I leave this dock with a calm and quiet conscience. My lord, I thank you for your kindness in allowing me to say these few words.*

Lord Chief Justice *– Prisoner at the bar, you have been found guilty, in my opinion upon the clearest and most conclusive evidence, of the murder of Harriet Louisa Lane, which has been laid to your charge. No one, I think, who has heard this trial can entertain the slightest shadow of a doubt of your guilt, and I can only deplore that, standing as you surely are upon the brink of eternity, you should have called God to witness the rash assertion which has just issued from your lips. There can be no doubt that you took the life of this poor woman, who had been on the closest and most intimate terms of familiarity and affection with you, who had been the mother of your children. You inveigled her into the lone warehouse. The revolver was not there before, but it must have been taken in for the purpose, and with that she was slain. The grave was dug there for her remains, which were those you were removing when you were arrested; and about that no one can entertain the shadow of a doubt. It was a barbarous, cruel, inhuman, and cowardly act. I do not wish to say* *anything to aggravate the position in which you stand, nor dwell upon the enormity of your guilt, further than by way of rousing you to a sense of the position which you now occupy, in which the hope of earthly mercy is cut off. The only hope and consolation you can have is in the future, where truth cannot be mistaken, where no assertion of yours will stand you in any stead, though where, if you seek for mercy, it must be through sincere repentance from the crime which you have undoubtedly committed. I have to warn you against any delusive hope of mercy here as long as the law exists which say that he who takes the life of a fellow-creature with malicious afterthought shall answer for it with his own. This is a case to which it would be impossible that mercy could be extended, therefore, prepare for the doom which awaits you. I have now only to pass upon you the dreadful sentence of the law, which is that you be taken from hence to the place whence you came, thence to a legal place of execution, to be there hanged by the neck till you shall be dead; that your body be buried within the precincts of the gaol in which you shall be last confined after your conviction; and may the Lord have mercy upon your soul.*

The Lord Chief Justice then turned his attention to Thomas Wainwright:

Lord Chief Justice – *Thomas George Wainwright, the jury have, in my opinion correctly, acquitted you of the heavier crime of having entered into the scheme conceived by your brother with a view to the murder of Harriet Lane. Their opinion, and they have pronounced it by their verdict, is that, having become aware of the crime committed by your brother, you lent yourself to assist him in its concealment. No fraternal affection, no regard or sympathy which one brother should have for another, can excuse you in the eyes of the law for assisting in his endeavour to escape the consequences of justice. Your offence, although lighter, and one far short of being an accessory before the act, is one which ought to be punished with proper severity; for through the concealment of such crimes they have sometimes been perpetrated with impunity and safety, and human life thereby endangered. I am ready to believe that you were actuated under the influence which your brother had over you, without which you might not have done what you did. I have taken that into consideration, as I believe you have been his dupe and his tool, and he has in some degree your crime to answer for practically as well as his own. You yielded weakly and wrongly to his influence and his greater age; but although that does not in any way mitigate the character of the*

The Execution of Henry Wainwright at Newgate on 21 December 1875. Illustrated Police News

offence, I think, on the whole, that justice will not be satisfied with a less punishment than I am about to inflict. The sentence of the Court is that you be imprisoned and kept in penal servitude for seven years.

After the prisoners had been removed from the bar, the Lord Chief Justice said:

I think it right to exercise a power which I have vested in me, sitting here upon this trial, by Act of Parliament, to order that a reward be given from the proper fund to the man Stokes. His conduct and his energy on the occasion of these remains being removed from Whitechapel to the Borough, and his perseverance in following up the cab in which those remains were being conveyed, have in reality led to the discovery of this crime and the conviction of the offenders concerned in it. I shall direct, therefore, that he shall receive from the proper fund the sum of £30.

Henry Wainwright chose the hymns for the service in the prison chapel on his last Sunday. On the evening before his execution within Newgate Prison, he strolled up and down the yard in the company of the Governor of the prison, Mr Sydney Smith, smoking a cigar, allowed as a special privilege, while he recounted tales of his amorous adventures with numerous women. On the morning of his execution, Tuesday, 21 December 1875, Wainwright stepped briskly from his cell, nodded cheerily to the Governor and strode to the execution shed with a smile on his lips. He smile faded when he beheld the unexpected crowd of spectators, because the execution itself was only nominally private as some

William Marwood, who executed Henry Wainwright, was appointed executioner at Newgate in 1874 on the retirement of his predecessor, William Calcraft. He served as the nation's official executioner until he retired in 1888, and found the key to successful hanging was the 'long drop'. Author's collection

sixty-seven persons were present, admitted by special permission of the sheriff. There were unsubstantiated rumours that several women, disguised as men, were present. Wainwright's executioner was William Marwood who had only recently taken up his post in London. As Wainwright entered the execution shed, he said to the assembled company 'Come to see a man die have you, you curs?'

Following his execution, towards the middle of the day, the body of Henry Wainwright was placed in a rough deal box, filled with wood shavings and quick-lime, then carried by warders to a narrow, bleak gaol pathway, below massive gross-barred gratings, which almost shut out the light of day, which connected Newgate to the adjoining Sessions House. This grim corridor was known as Birdcage Walk but was more commonly referred to as Dead Man's Walk. Wainwright was buried there beneath the flagstones. The initial letters of the surnames of those buried there were carved into the wall, marking the spot beneath which they lay. This corridor was seldom visited, except by those who would walk down it on their way to their own execution.

In the aftermath of the trial and execution of Henry Wainwright, a collection raised £1,200 for Mrs Wainwright and her children. Exactly what happened to 'Mr and Mrs King's' two little girls is not recorded. Miss Ellen Wilmore said at the trial 'I have still got the children.' Whether Miss Wilmore continued to look after them is a matter of conjecture. It has been suggested that they could have been taken to the workhouse and conveniently forgotten. When Newgate was demolished in 1902, the remains of the ninety-seven executed prisoners recorded to have been buried in Dead Man's Walk, including those of Henry Wainwright, were lifted and reburied in the City of London Cemetery.

The Whitechapel Road of the present day retains many of the elements that were present during Wainwright's day. The sites involved in the case are easily identifiable, although Wainwright's shop and the Pavilion Theatre are long since gone, and the street numbering is entirely different. The theatre was badly damaged by fire and re-opened in 1894, as a Yiddish theatre. It suffered bomb damage during World War Two and ended its days as a cinema before it was finally demolished in 1962. Vine Court, the *Royal Oak* (no longer a public house) and Wainwright's warehouse still exist, although the appearance of the building has changed in the intervening years, its proportions fronting Whitechapel Road are substantially the same as in Wainwright's day.

CHAPTER 5

Jack the Ripper
1888

The mutilation of the body was of such a character as could only have been effected by a practised hand.

'The Whitechapel Murderer' was the original title accorded to the unknown 'Jack the Ripper'. In reality, although his murders occurred within one square mile, they strayed outside Whitechapel proper to Spitalfields. Five murders are known to have been committed by the Ripper, some accounts credit him with six murders, and the general public of the day believed that a seventh Whitechapel murder was the work of the Ripper. The case of Jack the Ripper was never solved.

Before, during and after the 1880s, the streets around much of the East-End were frequented by gangs who made their living from robbing, mugging and extortion. A notorious group who sometimes frequented the Whitechapel and Spitalfields area was the Nichol gang, so-called because the gang originated from Old Nichol Street, situated to the north of Bethnal Green Road. The first of the two murders not officially attributed to the Ripper, although in the opinion of the general public, it was a Ripper murder, was committed in Osborn Street, at its union with Brick Lane, outside Taylor Brothers' cocoa factory, during the early hours of 3 April 1888. The victim was an ageing prostitute called Emma Smith, who lived at 18 George Street, Spitalfields. She survived her terrible ordeal long enough to be able to describe what had occurred, and gave a description of her assailants. Apparently, three or four young men had followed her from Whitechapel High Street, and she described one as being no older than nineteen. They set about her, beat her up and raped her, before one of them thrust a blunt stick into her vagina, with such force that it tore the perineum. Her face and neck had also suffered cuts. She was taken to the London Hospital on Whitechapel Road, but having lapsed into unconsciousness, never recovered and died four days later. The police believed that members of the Nichol gang were responsible for this murder. However, when other prostitutes were murdered in the Whitechapel area later that year, many people linked Emma Smith's murder with the others.

Another Whitechapel murder that the general public of the time, and some criminologists, have attributed to the Ripper, took place during the August Bank Holiday of 1888. At 3 am on 7 August, the body of thirty-five-year-old Martha Tabram (or Turner), was found on a staircase landing in Commercial Street. Her throat had been cut and her body had been stabbed or pierced thirty-nine times with a long, sharp instrument, possibly a bayonet.

Police investigations revealed that Martha and a fellow prostitute, Mary Ann Connolly, known as 'Pearly Poll' had picked up a couple of soldiers the previous evening. Pearly Poll had gone off with her soldier and they had left Martha and her client at about midnight near George Yard. Pearly Poll said that one of the soldiers was a corporal. All non-commissioned officers and privates who had been granted leave on Bank Holiday night were put into an identity parade at the garrison at the Tower of London, but Pearly Poll failed to pick the two soldiers out. Afterwards she remembered that the soldiers were wearing white caps, which identified them as Coldstream Guards. So, Pearly Poll was taken to Wellington Barracks and an identity parade was held there. She proved to be uncooperative with the authorities and a most unreliable witness. At the second identity parade she simply picked out two soldiers at random. Both had cast iron alibis. Other possible suspects were eliminated and the police believed that this murder may have been simply another committed by the blackmailing gangs of extortionists. The name of the Hoxton 'Hi-Rips' was mentioned, bringing the word 'ripping' into Whitechapel murder terminology in 1888.

Just twenty-four hours after the death of Martha Tabram, the first accepted victim of Jack the Ripper was murdered in Buck's Row (today's Durward Street) at about 3.30 am on Friday, 31 August, forty-two-year-old prostitute, Mary Ann Nichols (known as Polly), was found lying on her back. Her throat had been cut twice from left to right, the second, eight inch long cut had been inflicted with such severity that it had severed the jugular vein, trachea and half her spinal column, almost removing her head. Her face was bruised. After her body had been removed to the mortuary by the old Montague Street workhouse, the full extent of her injuries was realised. A large gash ran from the bottom of the ribs to the pelvis. The stomach lining had been slashed and there were two stabs to the genitals.

The policemen carrying out their investigations in the district of Whitechapel, like the general public, considered this to be the third 'Ripper' murder, but, two years later, those in authority decided that the murder of Polly Nichols was the first murder committed in Whitechapel by the criminal known as 'Jack the Ripper.'

The next murder took place on Saturday, 8 September. At 6 o'clock that morning, the body of forty-five-year-old prostitute, Annie Chapman, was found in the back yard of 29 Hanbury Street. The front door of No. 29 opened into a narrow passageway that led right through the house to the back door and to the small back yard beyond. The house was sub-let to a variety of tenants and both the front and back doors were left unlocked to allow the lodgers to come and go as they pleased. Seventeen people slept at No.29, yet nobody saw or heard the Ripper.

Annie Chapman, also known as Dark Annie, Annie Siffey or Sievey (she had once lived with a man who made sieves), lay on her back with her knees apart and her black skirt pushed up over them, she was wearing a pair of red and white striped stockings. Her face was swollen and her chin and jaw were bruised. Her tongue protruded from her mouth. Two savage cuts to the neck had almost severed the head and her stomach had been torn open and sections of skin from

Annie Chapman, murdered in Hanbury Street on Saturday, 8 September. The Illustrated Police News

the stomach lay on her left shoulder. The right shoulder was similarly adorned with a piece of skin and a quantity of small intestines. In fact Annie Chapman had been disembowelled. It was later discovered that her bladder, uterus and part of her vagina had been removed and taken away by the Ripper. Her rings, three of them, made of brass, had also been torn from her fingers and some pennies, two new farthings and a comb lay by the body.

In his evidence at the inquest, George Bagster Phillips, surgeon, stated:

> *The mutilation of the body was of such a character as could only have been effected by a practised hand. It appears that the abdomen had been entirely laid open; that the intestines, severed from their mesenteric attachments had been lifted out of the body, and placed by the shoulder of the corpse; whilst from the pelvis the uterus and its appendages, with the upper part of the vagina and the posterior two-thirds of the bladder, had been entirely removed. No trace of these parts could be found, and the incisions were cleanly cut, avoiding the rectum, and dividing the vagina low enough to avoid injury to the cervix uteri. Obviously the work was that of an expert – of one, at least, who had some knowledge of anatomical or pathological examination as to be enabled to secure the pelvic organs with one sweep of a knife, which must therefore, as Mr Phillips pointed out, have been a least five inches long.*

The next victim of Jack the Ripper was also killed in a yard. This was the night of 30 September, when the then much talked about 'two in one night' Ripper murders took place. It was a wet and windy night. In the back yard of 40 Berners Street (now Henriques Street), a turning south of Commercial Road, backed on to by a Jewish Socialist Club, the body of Elizabeth Stride (a Swede, whose maiden name was Gustafsdotter), also known as Long Liz, was found. Louis Diemschutz, was a hawker who also worked as a steward at the club. As he drove into the yard in a pony and trap the horse shied and Diemschutz's attention was drawn to what he thought was a heap of clothes on the ground. He soon discovered otherwise and went to fetch help from the club.

Long Liz was lying on her left side with her legs drawn up and her right arm over her stomach. Her left arm was extended behind her back, the hand of which was clutching a piece of tissue paper containing cachous. A check silk scarf around her neck concealed the gash in her throat, which ran from left to right and had penetrated to

The 'two in one night' murders of Elizabeth Stride and Catherine Eddowes. The Illustrated Police News

a depth of three inches. There was bruising to her neck and face, which suggested that she had been forced down to the ground before her throat was cut. It seems that the murderer had been prevented from carrying out any further mutilation and made his escape as he heard the approaching pony and trap.

Around the same time that Elizabeth Stride's body was discovered, another prostitute, Catherine Eddowes, aged forty-three, was being released from Bishopsgate Police Station, where she had been taken in a drunken state earlier that evening. She lived at 6 Fashion Street with her common-law husband, John Kelly, and was known by some people as Kate Kelly. After she left the police station she made her way to Mitre Square, where a little over half-an-hour later she was laying dead. Police constable Watkins, who found the body, said that his beat took between ten and fourteen minutes to patrol. When he walked through Mitre Square at 1.30 am and shone his bull's-eye lantern into the various dark corners and alleyways, he saw nothing unusual. At 1.44 am he returned to Mitre Square. This time when he shone his lantern he saw the body of a woman lying in a corner. He later commented, 'The body had been ripped open like a pig in the market.'

Catherine Eddowes was laying on her back, her left leg was extended and her right one bent. Her throat had been savagely cut and there were several abrasions to both cheeks. Her face had been slashed and mutilated. There was a cut about a quarter of an inch through the lower left eyelid, dividing the structures completely through. The right eyelid was cut through to about half an inch. There was a deep cut over the bridge of the nose extending down near to the angle of the jaw on the right side of the cheek. Part of the nose and her right ear had been sliced off. The trunk had been cut open from the sternum to the groin and the victim had been disembowelled, her entrails having been thrown over her right shoulder. The uterus and the left kidney had been cut out and taken away.

When the body arrived at Golden Lane Mortuary, Detective Constable Halse noticed that part of the victim's apron was missing. It was found, at 2.55 am, in the doorway of 108–119 Wentworth Dwellings, Goulston Street (north-east of Mitre Square), covered with blood and bodily fluids. Chalked on the wall there was a message:

The Juwes are
The men That
Will not
be blamed
for nothing

PC Long who had discovered the piece of apron, said it had not been there at 2.20 am when he had patrolled the area, nor had the five line chalked message. Sir Charles Warren (Commissioner of the Metropolitan Police) arrived at Goulston Street at around 5.00 am and he ordered that the message should be rubbed out. Unfortunately, no photographs were taken of this potentially important clue. Warren later stated that he ordered its removal because he did not wish to exacerbate the anti-semitic feelings, which were rife at that time. Nor did he have the men available to deal with a 'racial riot.' There was a large Jewish population living in the streets where the Ripper murders had taken place and several suspects were themselves Jews.

The Times reported on 1 October 1888:

Two more murders must now be added to the blacklist of similar crimes of which the East End has very lately been the scene. The circumstances of both of them bear a close resemblance to those of the former atrocities. The victim in both has been a woman. In neither can robbery have been the motive, nor can the deed be set down at the outcome of an ordinary street brawl. Both have unquestionably been murders deliberately planned, and carried out by the hand of some one who has been no novice to the work. It was early yesterday morning that the bodies of the two women were discovered at places within a quarter of an hour's walk of one another, and at intervals of somewhat less than an hour. The first body was found lying in a yard in Berner – street, a low thoroughfare running out of the Commercial–road. The discovery was made about 1 o'clock in the early morning by a carter who was entering the yard to put up his cart. The body was that of a woman with a deep gash on the throat, running almost from ear to ear. She was quite dead, but the corpse was still warm, and in the opinion of the medical experts who were promptly summoned to the place, the deed of blood must have been done not so many minutes before. The probability seems to be that the murderer was interrupted by the carter... The body has been identified as that of Elizabeth Stride, a widow according to one account, according to another a woman living apart from her husband, and by all accounts belonging to the 'unfortunate' class...She left her house in Dean–street,

Spitalfields, between 6 and 7 o'clock on Saturday evening, saying that she was not going to meet anyone in particular. From that hour there is nothing certainly known about her up to the time at which her body was found, lifeless indeed, but not otherwise mutilated than by the gash in the throat, which had severed the jugular vein and must have cause instantaneous death …

… Not so the corpse of the second victim. In this case the purpose of the murderer had been fulfilled, and a mutilation inflicted of the same nature as that upon the body of Annie Chapman. It was in the south-western corner of Mitre-square, in Aldgate that the second body was found… in this instance the face had also been so slashed as to render it hard for the remains to be identified…The deed of blood had been the work of a practised hand. The body bore clear proof of some anatomical skill, but the murderer had been in a hurry, and had carried out his designs in a more rough fashion than that with which Annie Chapman's body had been mutilated. The best chance of identification seems to be from the victim's dress, of which a minute description has been put out.

When the above article appeared in *The Times,* Catherine Eddowes had not been identified as the victim. Experts who have examined the evidence suggest that the Ripper employed the same method when he killed Polly Nichols, Annie Chapman, Elizabeth Stride and Catherine Eddowes, in as much, that he seized the women from behind, with his left hand forcing the chin upwards as he grasped the face firmly, to expose the throat. The bruises on the faces of the victims suggested that he held them with considerable force, which would stifle any cries. Then taking his long bladed knife, he would cut the throat from left to right. In each case the victim was somewhat the worse for drink, which would have no doubt aided the Ripper in his task, as his victims were far from being alert.

Following this double murder on 30 September, panic spread through the streets of Whitechapel. Mischievous pranksters chalked messages in various places purporting to have come from the murderer and some sent letters to the police. On 3 October a letter and a postcard, received by the Central News Agency, were published with the permission of the police. The letter and the postcard that followed it gave the murderer a name. The letter was dated 25 September and posted on the 27th. It was addressed to: 'The Boss, Central News Office. London City.' It read:

Dear Boss

 I keep on hearing that the police have caught me but they wont fix me just yet. I have laughed when they look so clever and talk about being on the right track. That joke about Leather Apron gave me real fits. I am down on the whores and I shant quit ripping them till I do get buckled. Grand work the last job was. I gave the lady no time to squeal. I love my work and want to start again. You will soon hear of me with my funny little games. I saved some of the proper red stuff in a ginger beer bottle over the last job to write with but it went thick like glue and I cant use it. Red ink is fit enough I hope ha ha. The next job I do I shall clip the ladys ears off and send to the police officers just for jolly wouldn't you. Keep this letter back till I do a bit more work, then give it out straight. My knife's nice and sharp I want to get away right away If I get a chance. Good luck.
yours truly
Jack the Ripper

Don't mind me giving the trade name
Wasn't good enough to post this before I got all
The red ink off my hands curse it. No luck yet.
They say I'm a doctor now ha ha.

The postcard, also addressed to the Central News Office, was postmarked 1 October, the day after the double murder. It read:

I wasn't codding dear old Boss when I gave you the tip, youll hear about saucy Jackys work tomorrow double event this time number one squealed a bit couldn't finish straight off. had no time to get ears for police thanks for keeping last letter back till I got to work again.
Jack the Ripper

On Tuesday, 16 October, a small parcel, wrapped in brown paper and containing a cardboard box, was sent to a house in Alderney Street, Mile End. This was the home of a builder, George Lusk, who was Chairman of the Whitechapel Vigilance Committee. Inside the cardboard box was a letter and a human kidney. The letter was addressed: 'From Hell'. It read:

Sor I send you half the kidne I took from one woman prasarved it for you tother piece I fried and ate it was very nise I may send you the bloody knif that took it out if you only wate a whil longer.
signed Catch me when you can
Mishter Lusk

George Lusk and members of the Whitechapel Vigilance Committee examining the human kidney and letter, sent to them by post. The Penny Illustrated Paper and Illustrated Times

The authenticity of the kidney sent to George Lusk has been the subject of considerable speculation. Many commentators believe it to have been sent by medical students as a prank. The letter that accompanied the kidney was in an entirely different hand to the letter and postcard signed Jack the Ripper.

On 9 November the most appalling and brutal of all the Ripper murders took place. This was the only occasion when the Ripper was able to carry out his butchery indoors, and on this final occasion he had the luxury of time on his side. His victim was twenty-four-year-old Mary Jane Kelly (or Marie Jeanette or Mary Ann, as some accounts refer to her), otherwise known as Dark Mary. She had been murdered during the early hours of Friday, 9 November, in the back downstairs room of 26 Dorset Street. This was Mary's own room in the house, known as No. 13 McCarthy's Rents. It had been partitioned off from the rest of the house and had its own entrance, a side door that opened onto a passage, Miller's Court.

The landlord was John McCarthy who ran a small grocery business just outside Miller's Court at 27 Dorset Street. Her body was discovered at about 10.45 am by Thomas Bowyer, Mr McCarthy's

Mary Kelly lets Jack the Ripper into No. 13 McCarthy's Rents in Miller's Court. The Penny
Illustrated Paper and Illustrated Times

assistant, who had been sent to collect the outstanding rent, which
amounted to the considerable sum of thirty-five shillings. Bowyer
went to the door but found it locked. He then went to the window,
where a broken pane enabled him to push back the coat that was

The last victim of Jack the Ripper, Mary Jane Kelly. The Illustrated Police News

hanging there. What he saw was the most horrendous sight. He went to tell his boss, who immediately accompanied him back to No. 13. McCarthy then told Bowyer to say nothing and sent him to fetch the police. Chief Inspector Beck was chatting to Detective Walter Dew (who was later to write an autobiography in 1938 entitled *I Caught Crippen*), in the Commercial Street Police Station, when Bowyer burst in. He called out 'Another one! Jack the Ripper! Awful! Jack McCarthy sent me.'

Beck and Dew, along with two uniformed police constables, accompanied Bowyer back to Miller's Court. When they pulled back the coat at the window, this is what they saw:

The poor woman lay on her back, entirely naked. Her throat was cut from ear to ear, right down to the spinal column. The ears and nose had been clean cut off. The breasts had also been cleanly cut off and placed on a table which was by the side of the bed. The stomach and abdomen had been ripped open, while the face was slashed about, so that the features of the poor creature were beyond all recognition. The kidneys and heart had also been removed from the body and placed on the table by the side of the breasts. The liver had likewise been removed and laid on the right thigh. The lower portion of the body and the uterus had been cut out, and these appeared to be missing. The clothes of the woman were lying by the side of the bed, as though they had been taken off and laid down in the usual manner.

The above account is taken from the agency report which appeared in various newspapers. Apparently the report was not absolutely accurate, as Mary Kelly was wearing a chemise or some linen undergarment, but the state of the remains at that dreadful scene of butchery caused those present to describe the body as naked. Joseph Barnett, a fish porter, who had lived with her for eighteen months, until two weeks previously, was able to identify the remains as being those of Mary Kelly by the eyes and ears.

This was Jack the Ripper's final Whitechapel Murder. Nobody knows who the Ripper was. The case was never solved. Of the many suspects , some were questioned but nobody seemed to fit the profile exactly.

The grandson of Sir Charles Warren, the Metropolitan Police Commissioner, said that his grandfather believed the Ripper 'to be a sex

The body of Mary Jane Kelly is removed from her home through Miller's Court. The Illustrated Police News

Following the murder of Mary Jane Kelly, Jack the Ripper's last victim, several witnesses came forward with descriptions of suspects. The Illustrated Police News

maniac who committed suicide after the Miller's Court murder – possibly the young doctor who was found in the River Thames on December 31 1888.' This young doctor was in fact thirty-one-year-old Montague John Druitt. His involvement in the murders has been a popularly held belief by many who have shown an interest in the Ripper case. He came from a medical family, but was not in fact a doctor himself but a failed barrister. Apparently he suffered from mental health problems and committed suicide. Some believe he did so because of the self realisation that he was insane. Chief Detective Inspector Abberline, who was the senior Scotland Yard detective investigating the Ripper case, thought George Chapman was the murderer. George Chapman (his real name was Severin Klosowski), then aged twenty-three, was a hairdresser's assistant in Whitechapel at the time of the Ripper murders in 1888. Chapman was hanged on 7 April 1903, for poisoning three women. The theory was that Chapman had changed his mode of killing for fear of detection. Abberline apparently said to the officer who arrested Chapman, 'You've got Jack the Ripper at last!' However, other detectives who worked closely on the case did not have the same opinion as Abberline. There was also a Royal suspect. The Duke of Clarence, Prince Eddie, eldest son of the Prince of Wales, who died prematurely in 1892, was suspected in some quarters of being Jack the Ripper. However, these unsubstantiated stories did not start circling until after his death. There were also rumours that the Ripper murders had links with Freemasonry. Another suspect was a Polish Jew, name Kominski. He hated women, especially prostitutes and was said to have strong homicidal tendencies. He was admitted to a lunatic asylum early in 1889. Yet another suspect was a Russian doctor and convict, who was considered a homicidal maniac and often detained in a lunatic asylum. His whereabouts at the time of the Ripper murders were not known His name was Michael Ostrog. Finally, more recently, due to the discovery of a sensational diary, James Maybrick, a Liverpool businessman, was considered a possible contender. Maybrick was himself murdered by his wife. He died of arsenical poisoning on 11 May 1889. As we saw at the beginning of this chapter, the case of the 'Whitechapel Murderer' known as 'Jack the Ripper' was never solved. I rather think that we will never find out the identity of this most notorious East End murderer.

CHAPTER 6

Rival Butchers Fight in Whitechapel
1893

'I found I was stabbed. I called out "I am killed outright!"' At this point the courtroom erupted into fits of laughter.

O n Tuesday, 7 March 1893 an altercation in Whitechapel resulted in the arrest of seventeen-year-old Charles Kershenberg, a Jewish butcher, unable to speak English, who was in the employ of a female butcher. He was charged with

Charles Kershenberg attacking Jacob Solomon, while his employer looks on. The Illustrated Police News

maliciously causing bodily harm to Jacob Solomon, master butcher, of 76 Plummer's Row, Whitechapel. Solomon went to his competitors business premises as he alleged she had accused him of taking away her customers. According to the evidence given in the police court, Solomon accused Kershenberg's employer of selling bad meat. Kershenberg sprang to his employer's defence, when Solomon allegedly tried to strike her, he having first accused her of taking customers from him. It was alleged Kershenberg struck Solomon.

Solomon, who had a wound close to his left eye, stated in his evidence 'I found I was stabbed. I called out "I am killed outright!"'

At this point the courtroom erupted into fits of laughter.

It was further alleged that Kershenberg had a knife in his hand when he struck Solomon, who also received a blow in the eye and was kicked. A witness stated that he saw Kershenberg draw a knife from under his apron and stab Solomon. A constable gave evidence that a doctor had stated that Solomon had been stabbed with a knife similar to one produced in court. In defence of Kershenberg it was stated that when Solomon tried to strike the woman, all Kershenberg did was to strike him. The magistrate, Mr Mead, considered the evidence and decided that it was so contradictory that the case against the accused was dismissed.

CHAPTER 7

Kidnapping in Bethnal Green
1893

She was unconscious and had a bruise above her left temple. Mr Woodward called a park constable and the child was conveyed to Bethnal Green Infirmary.

An inquest was held at the Vestry Hall, Bethnal Green on Wednesday, 17 May 1893, Mr Alfred Hodgkinson, the Deputy Coroner for North East London, presided. The hearing concerned the death of Mary Ellen Barnes, aged two and a half years.

Mary Barnes was the daughter of Mrs & Mrs George T Barnes of 2, Tuscan Street, Bethnal Green. George Barnes worked as a wood machinist. On Tuesday, 2 May, Mary was left playing in the passage of the house, when she suddenly disappeared. An extensive search was made for her but her whereabouts were not discovered until that night, when she was found in Bethnal Green Infirmary.

Charles Woodward, a labourer employed at Victoria Park, had found a little girl at about a quarter-past seven that evening, in the plantation near the guinea-pig house. She was unconscious and had a bruise above her left temple. Mr Woodward called a park constable and the child was conveyed to Bethnal Green Infirmary. The police were informed of the child's discovery. Mr Woodward said, although he had been working in the vicinity he had not noticed the child, either on her own, or with anyone else, until he had spotted her lying in the plantation.

On discovering his daughter in the Infirmary, George Barnes was told by Dr Knox, the medical superintendent, to take Mary home and keep her quiet. Dr Knox also advised Mr Barnes to seek further medical advice from a doctor once he had got the child home.

When questioned by her father, Mary said that an old man had taken her away and given her some tea. He had then robbed her of her earrings, her shoes and her cape. Following his daughter's tragic death, Mr Barnes said after he had collected Mary from the Infirmary she had not complained about feeling ill, nor had she said anything about the old man ill treating her. The following morning,

Little Mary Barnes being robbed by an 'old man'. The Illustrated Police News

Friday, 19 May, Dr Holland, of 190, Green Street, was called to attend on Mary. On his arrival he found the child was having convulsions. She was suffering from inflammation of the membranes of the brain, brought about by the injury to her head, and fright. Her conditioned gradually deteriorated and she died on Saturday morning.

Dr Styles, divisional surgeon of police, on the coroner's orders made a post-mortem examination of the body. He found a bruise over the left eye. In his opinion death was due to meningitis, accelerated by a blow, and the congestion was most apparent on the spot corresponding with the bruise. Inspector Helson said that extensive enquiries had been made but the police had been unable to find any witnesses or discover any clue that could establish who the man was that took Mary away. After a lengthy hearing the jury returned a verdict of 'Wilful murder by some person or persons unknown.'

POVERTY-AT-THE-EAST-END.

This illustration appeared in The Illustrated Police News *on Saturday 16 January 1892. It depicts the tragic scene of poverty stricken, immigrant parents, desperately hoping for a better outcome, as the doctor attends their undernourished, dying, baby daughter.* The Illustrated Police News

CHAPTER 8

Coffee-House Keeper Slays his Wife and Stepson, then Shoots Himself
1893

A five-chambered revolver was at her feet and she was dead. Morgan was seated on the right-hand side of the bed and was bleeding profusely.

Maud Austin was employed as a servant at the residence of Mr and Mrs Thomas Morgan, situated above Mr Morgan's business premises at 17, Amhusrt Road, Hackney. Mr Morgan was the proprietor of a coffee-house. He was aged fifty-six and lived with his wife of four years, Emma, aged forty-eight, and her son from a previous marriage, Arthur George Jennings, aged fourteen years and eleven months. As well as the Morgan's domestic servants, there were also two lodgers living in the house.

On Monday, 23 May 1893, Maud was out until ten o'clock in the evening. On arriving home she said goodnight to her employers and went to bed with her fellow servant. She was awakened just over three hours later at a quarter-past one on Tuesday morning, by the ringing of the bell in their room. On going downstairs she heard her master say 'Oh' several times. The door to Mrs and Mrs Morgan's bedroom was locked but she noticed that Arthur Jennings's door was ajar and on looking inside saw his lifeless body lying on the bed covered in blood. The lodgers appeared on the scene but retreated to their rooms as they declined to become involved. Maud rushed downstairs and into the street where she eventually chanced upon a police sergeant, who accompanied her back to the Morgan's house.

Police Sergeant Albert Cornish was called to 17, Amhurst Road at one-thirty on Tuesday morning. He first went to Arthur Jennings' room. On seeing the boy was dead, Sergeant Cornish went to the door of Morgan's room and forced it open. On entering the room he saw that Mrs Morgan was lying with her feet towards the foot of the bed. She was upon her stomach and a pillow was over her head. A five-chambered revolver was at her feet and she was dead. Morgan

Main Picture: *Sergeant Cornish shines his torch on the body of Emma Morgan and the recumbent Thomas Morgan, while Maud Austin looks on.* **Top left:** *Thomas Morgan shoots his stepson Arthur Jennings.* **Top right:** *Thomas Morgan's coffee-house and the family home.* **Bottom right:** *The murderer and suicide victim, Thomas Morgan.* The Illustrated Police News

was seated on the right-hand side of the bed and was bleeding profusely.

Other policemen arrived on the scene, and so did Dr John White, of Portland Place, Clapton, the divisional surgeon, who said he found the dead boy in the front bedroom. There was a gunshot wound half-an-inch below the right ear. On the same floor in a back bedroom he found Mrs Morgan lying on her face. She had a gunshot wound in her left cheek. The bullet had passed into the mouth and shattered the right part of the jaw into several pieces. The woman had died from excessive bleeding. Surprisingly, nobody in the house had heard the sound of gunshots.

Thomas Morgan was lying on his back on the bed, next to his dead wife. He was groaning and appeared to be in considerable pain. Dr Whites' initial examination indicated that the injured man had a wound in the abdomen and another in the centre of the right thigh, below the groin. Dr White asked Mr Morgan who had killed the woman and the boy, and he replied, 'Yes, yes.' When he was asked if someone else did it, he replied 'Yes'. When the injured man answered 'Yes' to any question he was asked, Dr White realised that little importance could be attached to his replies.

Morgan was conveyed by ambulance to the German Hospital, accompanied by Sergeant Cornish. On the way Morgan said to him, 'I did it.' When they arrived at the hospital at about three o'clock, Morgan was examined by house surgeon Dr Herman Patersen, who in addition to the injuries described by Dr White, found there was another gunshot wound in the right thigh, but Dr Patersen believed that this was an exit wound.

Meanwhile, Inspector William Bond, in charge of Hackney district, who had been called to the crime scene, arriving at a quarter to two, examined the Smith and Weston revolver used in the shootings. All five chambers had been discharged and there were five empty cartridge cases in the revolver. No other cartridges were found at the scene.

On further examination in the operating theatre, it was discovered that Thomas Morgan's bowels had been perforated at least four times. The bullet could not be found in any of the patient's wounds. The bowels were sewn up and his other wounds attended to, but after the operation Morgan's temperature dropped dramatically. He did not last the night and died suddenly at about six o'clock. Dr Patersen said he had been unable to understand what the patient was saying when he tried to speak.

The inquest on the bodies of Mr and Mrs Morgan and Arthur Jennings was held before Alfred Hodgkinson, deputy coroner, at Hackney Coroner's Court on Thursday, 1 June 1893. Mr Hodgkinson stated at the beginning of the proceedings that he thought the evidence would establish the fact that the boy died first, then the woman, and that it was after her death that the man received the ultimate fatal injuries.

Thomas Morgan's sister, Mrs Susan Burham, of 68 Thurlow Street, Walworth, said that her brother had enjoyed good health up to July 1892. On the 17th of that month, he was seized with paralysis and the condition had affected his brain. She added she had last seen him three weeks before his death and that he was unable to speak much. She also remarked that her brother had made frequent complaints to her that his wife and stepson had been unkind to him.

Mrs Morgan's son-in law, Frederick James Hillman, a gardener, of 39 Alvington Street, Hornsey Rise, said that he had known Thomas Morgan for about four years, since he married his mother-in-law; and that he was a very nice gentleman, a good business man, and a kind father and husband. All this however, was changed after Mr Morgan had suffered a paralytic stroke and for no reason whatever he would get into most violent tempers. Mr Hillman said that earlier that year, on Whit Monday, he and his wife had met Mr and Mrs Morgan at the Manor Gates, Finsbury Park and from there had travelled to New Southgate. On the return journey, Mr Morgan became extremely disagreeable and proceeded to walk very fast, which Mr Hillman said he considered was too much for him. Then on the tramcar home, Mr Morgan slapped Mrs Morgan's face. Immediately following the slapping incident, Mr Hillman said that Mr Morgan pointed to a ring, pin and chain he was wearing, and then as he could not say anything more than 'Yes' to Mr Hillman, he took hold of his tongue and tried to tear it out. The party arrived back at Amhurst Road a little after eight o'clock and Mr Morgan had tea but he seemed to be in a very disagreeable mood. Mr Hillman said that Mrs Morgan would not give her consent to have her husband committed to a lunatic asylum, although papers had been partially drawn up.

Maud Austin said that during the three weeks she had been in service with the Morgans, Mr Morgan had behaved very badly to his wife. He frequently made use of the expression 'Damned scoundrel', and often when quietly seated at the table at meal times, he would suddenly fly into a passion and spit in the faces of all present. On Monday, 16 May, Miss Austin said that her master had thrown his wife down and attacked her with a knife. She had gone to her mistress's assistance and wrestled it away from him.

The jury returned a verdict of wilful murder against Thomas Morgan in the cases of Mrs Morgan and her son, and they found that he afterwards committed suicide while mentally deranged.

On Saturday, 31 June 1893 *The Illustrated Police News* reported:

On Saturday afternoon [27 May] *the three victims of the tragedy were interred in three separate strangers' graves in Ilford cemetery. The bodies had been left at the mortuary until the last moment. The coffins were all of polished elm, with massive fittings. The plates were inscribed as follows: – "Thomas Morgan died May 24th 1893. Aged fifty-four"; Emma Morgan, died May 23rd 1893. Aged forty-eight years; and "Arthur George Jennings, died May 23rd 1893. Aged fifteen years." At half past two three hearses, each drawn by a pair of horses wearing plumes, were driven into the churchyard in which the mortuary is situated , and the undertaker" men carried in a number of wreaths. The most noticeable was a huge cross, which was sent with "Deep sympathy from Arthur's young friends." There were a number of other wreaths, all sent either for the boy's or Mrs Morgan's coffin, but not one was sent to be placed on the man's coffin. The cortège proceeded via Amhurst-road, Pembury-road, and Mare-street to Lee-bridge-road, and thence to Ilford, where the burial service was read in the presence of a large concourse of people.*

CHAPTER 9

Tragedy in Hackney on Bonfire Night 1893

***... it was discovered that the bullet had struck him in
the chest, just above his heart.***

William Spiegelhalter and his younger brother John, aged
seventeen, the sons of a German clockmaker, of 405,
Hackney Road, had decided to join in the celebrations to
remember the fifth of November, with a pyrotechnic display of their
own. The fifth was a Sunday, and that evening a bonfire was lighted

*John Spiegelhalter firing a pistol on Bonfire Night 1893. A stray bullet strikes his
neighbour, Alfred Sawyer, in the chest.* The Illustrated Police News

at eight o'clock with the ubiquitous effigy of Guy Fawkes, placed on top of it and crackers discharged following the lighting of the fire. During the programme of events, pistol shots were introduced into the proceedings. For some reason it was thought necessary to load the pistol with live ammunition and fire it into the air. While William took care of the fireworks, John took charge of the pistol. There were several friends and relations in the Spiegelhalter's garden that night and the boy next door, Alfred Albert Sawyer, aged fifteen, living at No. 403, was watching the festivities with obvious delight, over the party wall.

John Spiegelhalter had fired the pistol and spent all five rounds. After going into the kitchen to re-load, he rushed out and discharged it with what was afterwards described as perfectly innocent intent. For a few moments no one was aware that anything seriously amiss had occurred. Unfortunately, a stray bullet had struck Alfred Sawyer and moments later he dropped to the ground. He was carried into the kitchen of his home, where it was discovered that the bullet had struck him in the chest, just above his heart. He died within a few minutes, before any medical help could be summoned, although there was little anyone could have done for him.

On realising what calamity had befallen their young neighbour, Mr and Mrs Spiegelhalter immediately ordered their son John to go to stay with relatives in Harlesden. Detective Inspector Nelson of J Division was quickly at the scene and went to the Sawyers's house, where he saw the dead boy lying on the kitchen floor. On establishing the facts from various witnesses and having obtained from the Spiegelhalters the address to which their son had been sent, a police officer was dispatched to Harlesden. On his arrival there, the officer arrested the terrified youth at midnight. John Spiegelhalter was detained at Harlesden Police Station on the Monday night, then brought to Bethnal Green on Tuesday, where he made an appearance at Worship Street Police Court, where he was charged with causing the death of Alfred Albert Sawyer by discharging a pistol. An inquest on the body of Alfred Albert Sawyer was held the following week and the jury returned a verdict of 'Death from misadventure.'

CHAPTER 10

William Seaman and the Turner Street Murders
1896

His throat had been cut from ear to ear with some sharp instrument, while the back of his skull had been battered in with what appeared, from the terrible nature of the wounds, to be a hammer. The features bore an agonised look, though it was later supposed that death must have come quickly.

Early on the afternoon of Saturday, 4 April 1896 the East End was plunged into a state of wild excitement by the harrowing details which came to hand of one of the most brutal double murders, accompanied by attempted burglary, that had been seen in Whitechapel since the Jack the Ripper murders of 1888. The scene of the outrage was 31, Turner Street, Commercial Road East. The victims were Mr John Goodman Levy, aged seventy-seven, a recently retired umbrella manufacturer, and his housekeeper, Anna Sarah Gale, a married woman, aged thirty-five. Until six weeks previously Mr Levy had carried on his business in the style of M J Myers but had handed the business over to his stepson, the offspring of his late wife's first marriage. As well as the legitimate trade Mr Levy had dealt in, there was a darker side to his business activities. There had been several attempted burglaries at Mr Levy's house previously, some quite recently and it was generally believed among the criminal fraternity that Levy kept the wealth he had amassed as a fence, on the premises.

The first suspicion of foul play was aroused a little before one o'clock on Saturday, when, Mrs Martha Lawton, a cousin of Mr Levy, who lived in the same street at No. 35, went to the house to keep a luncheon appointment. She had dined there the previous evening. No 31 was situated on the corner with Varden Street, where it had its entrance door. It was a three-storeyed, eight roomed house,

The site of 31 Turner Street, seen here in December 2004. No 31 is occupied by Wahab Tailors. The author

with a flat parapet, concealing its shallow roof from the street. Much to her astonishment, Mrs Lawton remained knocking at the door for some minutes without any response being forthcoming. A strange feeling crept over her that something was amiss inside the house. The loud and constant rapping attracted the attention of the next door neighbour, a tailor, named William Schafer, who came out to see what was the matter. Mrs Lawton told him that she could not make anyone hear at 31, and then suggested that he should go to his back yard and see if he could ascertain anything by getting on the partition wall. This Mr Schafer did by means of a ladder. On climbing the ladder Mr Schafer was astonished to see the head of a strange man in a brown cloth cap just inside the small window which gave a view of the narrow corridor leading to the doorway affording entrance from Varden Street. He shouted out to the stranger who immediately

A view of the houses immediately across the road from 31 Turner Street, (the home of Mr John Goodman Levy in 1896), on the opposite corner of Turner Street and Varden Street, seen here in December 2004. The photograph shows the corner house, No. 33 Turner Street. Like Mr Levys house, the entrance door is in Vardon Street. Mr Levy's house was built in exactly the same style as the houses seen here, except there was an additional storey. Mr Levy's cousin, Mrs Martha Lawton's house, No. 35, is next door. The author

disappeared from view. He reappeared shortly afterwards, clearly believing the coast was clear. However, the stranger was very much mistaken, as Mr Schafer had concealed himself behind the wall. The moment the man exposed himself, Mr Schafer called out to him and demanded to know what he was doing there. The man disappeared from view.

Growing increasingly suspicious that something was wrong, Mr Schafer hurried down the ladder and through his house into the street, with the intention of summoning the police. There he found other neighbours gathered outside No. 31. The constables on duty in the vicinity, having being summoned, were soon on the spot and Mr Schafer led two of them through his house, No. 29, to the partition wall, where they climbed the ladder and attempted to enter No. 31. Meanwhile, a careful watch was kept on both the front and back of the premises to prevent anyone escaping. The police were apprehensive as to what they might find, and enlisted the help of several passers by. The party then proceeded to search the premises. Half concealed behind the lavatory door at the back of the ground floor they discovered the body of Mr Levy, lying in a pool of blood. He was lying in a crouched position partly on his side, with his face turned upwards. His throat had been cut from ear to ear with some sharp instrument, while the back of his skull had been battered in with what appeared, from the terrible nature of the wounds, to be a hammer. The features bore an agonised look, though it was later supposed that death must have come quickly.

As the search of the house continued, the police found that drawers had been ransacked and overturned, and on the first floor, a safe in which Mr Levy kept items of considerable value, had been moved from its original position, evidently with the intention of it being forced from the back. In the back second floor bedroom, used by the housekeeper, another ghastly sight awaited the police. Mrs Gale lay on the floor, stretched out by the bedstead, in a pool of blood, which was streaming in all directions. Her head had been almost completely severed from her body, and the skull unmercifully beaten with a blunt instrument. The evidence at this particular murder scene suggested that, although taken by surprise, whilst making the bed, the housekeeper had fought fiercely for her life, for everything was in a state of wild disorder, while splashes of blood marked the walls.

In the front room of the second floor, the police officers noticed that a hole had been made in the ceiling giving access to the roof. The laths and plaster had been beaten in with a hammer, and an aperture made sufficiently large to enable a man to climb through.

While the search of the house was continuing, a strong contingent of police had arrived in Turner Street. One policeman on the scene was Detective Sergeant F P Wensley, who was later to become the first Assistant Commissioner promoted from the ranks. Just as the officers inside the house had discovered the hole in the ceiling, there was a loud cry from the street below that there was a man on the roof. A ladder was fetched to enable the police to gain access to the roof via the hole in the ceiling. Just as one constable had got his body half-way through the hole into the void to the roof, he caught sight of a man standing in the gutter which ran round the roof. Moments later the man had mounted the coping, hauled himself over by his hands, and dropped into the street below, a distance of between forty and fifty feet. As he fell, the man's body struck the back of a little girl, Leah Hyams, who was standing with her mother close under the wall at the Varden Street entrance to the house. The man was carrying two bundles with him, in which he had apparently collected his plunder. These parcels, on subsequently being examined by the police, were found to contain several gold watches, some rings, and other jewellery, as well as a quantity of money. Other items of value identified as belonging to the murder victims, were found concealed in the garments of the man.

As the man struck the pavement with a dull thud he was at once surrounded by police. However, the fall had rendered him insensible and he had sustained serious injuries. Constable Hacchus 359H, saw the man fall and was the first police office to get to him. He saw a gold chain and other valuable items fall from his pocket. The injured man was taken inside the house. Constable Hacchus, 359H, said, after carrying Seaman into the house a sum of 1s 3d was handed to him, as money that had been picked up by one of the crowd. An ambulance was fetched and between two and three o'clock the injured man was conveyed by constables to the London Hospital, where on his arrival he was attended to by Mr Lewis Smith, the senior house surgeon. Mr Smith ascertained that the man was suffering from concussion of the brain, a fractured right shoulder and injuries to the right leg. The man remained in an insensible condition throughout the night, and it was not until Sunday afternoon that he regained consciousness. Mr Lewis Smith commented on Sunday that the patient was in a very serious condition, though he entertained hopes of his recovery. He had permitted no one, not even the police, to see the man, as quietude was absolutely essential.

Little Leah Hyams was also picked up in an insensible condition and taken to a neighbour's house where restoratives were applied. On being brought round she was taken to the London Hospital where she received attention for injuries to her back and for fright. She was discharged from the hospital later that day. On Sunday afternoon,

The present-day Royal London Hospital, formerly known as the London Hospital, where Seaman received treatment for his injuries. The author

her parents said that Leah complained greatly of pains about the body, and was still suffering from fright.

Immediately upon the discovery of the bodies at 31 Turner Street, Dr Michael and Dr Ambrose, who had medical practices nearby, were sent for. So terrible was the nature of the wounds that had been inflicted on the murder victims that it was pronounced that death, in each case, must have been almost instantaneous. Evidence at the murder scene suggested that the murders took place sometime during the morning, probably after breakfast, as it was established that the victims had partaken of breakfast that morning. The police were at a loss to determine by what method the burglar affected an entrance to the house, for there was no evidence of a forced entry. The weapons with which the murders were perpetrated, consisted of a formidable-looking clasp knife and a heavy hammer. Both instruments were found in the course of Saturday afternoon on the roof. They were smeared with clotted blood and had apparently been dropped by the burglar in his hurried flight when discovered by the police.

On Saturday, 11 April *The Illustrated Policed News* reported:

... the man in custody at the London Hospital was on Sunday identified by Detective-inspector Marshall, of Scotland Yard, as one of a daring gang of burglars who have infested the metropolis for many years past. The officers in charge of the case refuse to divulge the name of the man, but he is known to the members of the Criminal Investigation Department under several aliases. The prisoner is a thick-set man, between 5ft 8in and 5ft 9in in height, with slightly bent shoulders and a small tuft of red whiskers under the chin. He has been engaged, it is said, in many notorious robberies, and has spent a considerable number of years in prison. On one occasion he was sentenced at the Old Bailey to penal servitude for robbery with violence, and he has undergone long terms of imprisonment for housebreaking in various parts of the country. That the dastardly murder in Turner Street was the work of the gang of thieves with which the prisoner had been so long identified has left little room for doubt amongst those officers engaged in the case. The fact that the murder was not the work of one man has also been clearly established after a minute examination of the house and the room where the murders were committed. The footprints in the attics and on the staircase clearly show that the man in custody was assisted in carrying out his nefarious work.

Up to Sunday evening the police had not succeeded in making any further arrest in connection with the murders.

On Saturday, 2 May 1896 *The Times* reported:

Yesterday morning, William Seaman, 46, described as a lighterman of Claud-street, Millwall, was brought from the London Hospital and charged at the Thames Police-court with the wilful murders of Sarah Annie Gale and John Goodman Levy, of 31, Turner-street, Whitechapel on the 4th ult. The prisoner was lifted into the Court seated on an armchair and was evidently suffering considerable pain. Seaman, who was undefended, was on Thursday night interviewed by Mr Bedford, solicitor, but declined that gentleman's services.

Mrs Alice Weidemann, of 88, Overstrand Mansions, Battersea Park, gave evidence She said she was the sister of the murdered woman and that her sister, Mrs Gale, was married but living apart from her husband; and had been acting as housekeeper to Mr Levy for ten or eleven years.

It transpired that on Sunday, 5 April, while Constable Hacchus and Constable Rutter were in charge of the prisoner at the hospital, Seaman spoke to Hacchus as he was endeavouring to give him some milk, Seaman said, 'Oh, I don't trouble much about that. I could go to the scaffold and swing for what I have done without fear. I know what is in front of me, and I can face it. If a man takes life he must suffer for it. I don't value my life a bit. I have made my bed. I must lie on it.'

Mr Lewis Smith, house surgeon at the London Hospital, said that when Mrs Bowater, Seaman's landlady, was called to identify him he said to her, 'I am guilty. I did it for revenge. He swindled me years ago. I did it for revenge.'

Constable G Bryan, 176H said, in his evidence given at Thames Police Court that, on 11 April while he was in charge of the prisoner at the London Hospital, Seaman said to him ' I suppose old Levy is dead by this time and buried? Constable Bryan told Seaman that he didn't know. Seaman went on 'I am glad I have done for him. I have been a good many times for the money, amounting to £70, and the old man always made some excuse. I made up my mind to do for him. I am not afraid of being hanged.' The next day on waking up Seaman said:

I have been a frequent visitor to the house in Turner Street, where the job was done; and if the old Jew had only paid me the £70, the job would not have happened. You do not know one-half of what there has been between old Levy and me. No one else knows it now, and I will keep it to myself. You do not know what I have had to put up with him; but this finishes the lot. That morning I knocked at the door, old Levy himself opened it, and I walked in. He said that the girl was upstairs. I then went upstairs and found her in the room. She had got her dress on and was leaning over the bed, which appeared to me not to have been slept in. When she saw me, she shouted and began struggling but I soon stopped her. I then came downstairs and put the old Jew's lights out. After the job was finished I heard someone knocking at the door. I stood behind the door considering whether to let them in or not. If I had opened the door I would soon have floored them, so as they would not have walked out of that house again alive. I then got onto the roof from the inside and saw my only chance was to dive from there head first. If it had not been for someone who broke my fall I should not have been living here now. I know I am going to get hung, and would not care if it was now, for I am tired of my life.' On another day he said 'I have been crushed ever since I was 19 years old. I have done 14 years and two sevens.'

Constable Elliott was present at the time.

On 17 April, Constable Hacchus was once again in charge of the prisoner, and whilst he was assisting in washing Seaman, the latter said, 'Never mind washing anything else, as I shan't be here long. I don't value my life. I want to die as soon as I can. I don't want to hide anything and I shan't try to. I did it. I have been prompted to do this thousands of times. I knew the old man had been the cause of all my trouble, and I would like to kill myself now. I am sick of my life.'

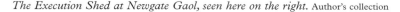

The Execution Shed at Newgate Gaol, seen here on the right. Author's collection

The feared triple gallows at Newgate, on which William Seaman was hanged between Albert Milsom and Henry Fowler, on 9 June 1896. Author's collection

The outcome of Seaman's trial at the Old Bailey was almost a foregone conclusion. Found guilty of wilful murder he was sentenced to death.

Seaman was hanged at Newgate on 10 June 1896, along with Albert Milsom and Henry Fowler, two habitual petty criminals who, during the course of a burglary in February 1896, had murdered seventy-nine-year-old, retired engineer, Henry Smith, of Muswell Lodge, Tetherdown, Muswell Hill in North London. At their trial held at the Old Bailey in May, apart from the clue of a toy lantern which proved crucial in identifying the murderers, and ensured the case attracted much coverage in the press (it was subsequently included in many true crime publications), this case is notable for the violent outburst as the jury returned with their guilty verdict. Fowler flung himself across the dock at Milsom and tried to strangle him, very nearly succeeding in saving the executioner the job of hanging

Milsom. At their execution Seaman was placed between Milsom and Fowler. Seaman's last words are reputed to be 'This is the first time I've ever been a bloody peacemaker.'

James Billington was the executioner. An unusual mishap occurred during the execution. Four warders were in close attendance on the scaffold. One of them obscured Billington's view of his assistant executioner, Warbrick. Warbrick was still pinioning the feet of one of the prisoners when Billington operated the lever that opened the trap door. The three criminals plummeted to their deaths as Warbrick was catapulted into the pit. Fortunately, he heard the bolt beneath him being withdrawn and instinctively grabbed the legs of the man in front of him. He ended up swinging below the feet of the three dead men. The execution of Seaman, Milsom and Fowler, was the last triple execution that took place at Newgate.

CHAPTER 11

Mysterious Death of a Reputed Bethnal Green Miser

1897

He then struck her a violent blow in the face with a short hammer, which he took from his outside coat pocket.

In September 1897, Peel Grove, Old Ford Road, was the focus of a police investigation, following the discovery of the mutilated body of seventy-one-year-old Miss Margaret Marshall at her home there. According to neighbours, Miss Marshall had lived at 10, Peel Grove for as long as anybody could remember. It was a quiet and respectable house, situated in an equally quiet and respectable neighbourhood. The murder victim had last been seen alive on Wednesday, 15 September.

On 23 October, *The Illustrated Police News,* reported an extraordinary development concerning investigations into Miss Marshall's death:

A curious story from Bethnal Green concerning the murder of Miss Marshall, is one of the undiscovered crimes which have recently shocked the metropolis. An extraordinary letter has been received by the coroner for North-east London, in which the writer, who professes to be clairvoyant, gives a graphic account of the crimes as revealed by that mystic art. The writer says:- "The murderer was a young man short in stature, and of fair complexion. His hair was light brown , and his eyes, which were somewhat prominent, were of a greyish hue. He was dressed in shabby clothes , the pockets of his jacket being of exceptional size. For some days previous to the murder he hung about Peel Grove, making himself well acquainted with Miss Marshall and her habits. On the night of the murder he watched the house for some time, and at ten o'clock walked deliberately up to the door and knocked. His knock was answered by Miss Marshall, who only partially opened the door, and inquired his business. He told her he came from the landlord with a message, and as

THE RECENT MURDER OF A WOMAN IN BETHNAL GREEN.
WILL A CLAIRVOYANT'S VISION HELP TO TRACE THE MURDERER?

On Saturday 23 October 1897 The Illustrated Police News *reported that a clairvoyant had described a vision he had experienced regarding the circumstances surrounding the unsolved murder of Miss Margaret Marshall in Bethnal Green.* The Illustrated Police News.

she opened the door wider, he sprung at her, seizing her by the throat with his left hand, and forcing her backwards into the passage. He then struck her a violent blow in the face with a short hammer, which he took from his outside coat pocket. The old lady gave a loud shriek, which seemed to alarm her assailant, who drawing a knife from his trousers pocket, stabbed her again and again. Her shrieks had struck terror into his soul, for he rushed from the house, banging the door behind him, and hurried away in a southerly direction.

The coroner intends to place the letter in the hands of the police, but whether the practical common-sense of Scotland Yard will place much reliance on a revelation which is based on clairvoyance in another matter.

I have been unable to find any record of what Scotland Yard made of the clairvoyant's assertions.

CHAPTER 12

Garrotting in the East End
1897 & 1899

*Dr Stonham said his head was held back, mouth
closed, and an arm passed round his neck.*

G arroting was an assault akin to mugging, in which a thief's victim was rendered insensible by pressing on the throat with fingers or a stick. A garrotta was a strangling strap used in Spain for execution. This new variation on the method of execution began in England in 1851 after news came of the execution of General Lopez in Havanah by order of the Spanish Government. On Saturday, 4 September 1897 *The Illustrated Police News* reported under the heading A MAN GARROTED IN A BUSY LONDON THOROUGHFARE:

Mr J. Mitchell of Leyton, was walking down the Mile End Road, when he was pushed into a side street opposite the London Hospital and pinioned by two burly ruffians. Two others then proceeded to tear away his trousers with the pocket in which he had his money. Great force was used, the trousers being literally torn away from top to bottom, leaving Mr Mitchell's legs naked. The thieves then appropriated Mr Mitchell's hat and made off.

The strange thing is that this was accomplished outside a shop, in which the victim took refuge and was supplied with an old pair of trousers to wear home. The police did not appear for some minutes afterwards, and the garroters [sic] *got clear away.*

On 1 July 1899 another garrotting incident was reported in *The Illustrated Police News* under the heading AN EAST-END DOCTOR GAROTTED [sic] AND ROBBED:

At the Thames Police Court, before Mr Cluer, Thomas Thompson and Henry Marsh, young men, were charged with being concerned with three others in assaulting and robbing Dr Henry A. Stonham, as well-known East-end doctor, living in Albert-square, of a gold watch, valued at £50.

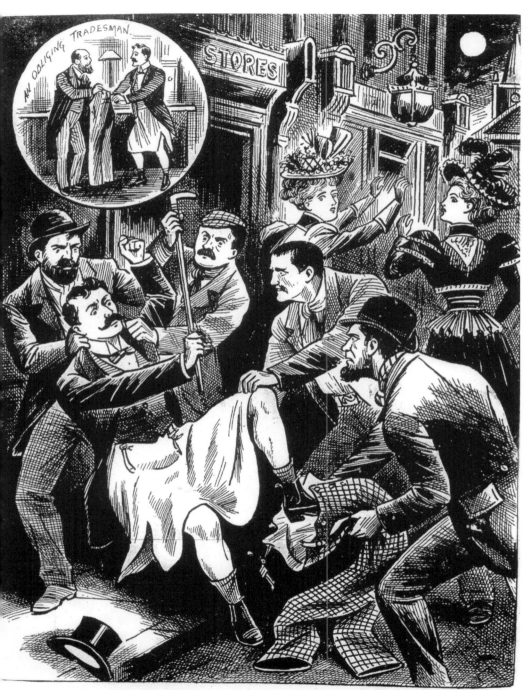

A MAN GARROTED IN A BUSY LONDON THOROUGHFARE.

Main Picture: *Mr Mitchell being garrotted by a gang in Mile End Road.* **Top left:** *An obliging tradesman supplies Mr Mitchell with a pair of trousers to wear for home.* Illustrated Police News.

Dr Stonham told the court that at about four o'clock on the afternoon of Thursday, 22 June, he was walking through Twine Court, Shadwell, after visiting a patient, when he was surrounded and seized by five men. Dr Stonham said his head was held back, mouth closed, and an arm passed round his neck. He was then robbed of a heavy gold watch, an heirloom that had been in his family for over a hundred years. A silver matchbox and some silver and some coppers were also taken. The doctor reported the incident to the police shortly afterwards.

Detective W Cridland of H Division, stated that on Tuesday, 27 June, in the company of Detective Richardson, he arrested

A scene from Newgate in 1872, as depicted in The Graphic. *A garrotter having been whipped with the 'cat of nine tails', is being assisted to put on his shirt.* The Graphic

Thompson, who said, 'I was there, but I did not assault him.' Detective Richardson reported this when Marsh was taken into custody he said, 'All right. Where did this take place?' On being told Marsh said, 'I know I was there, but I didn't rob him. If that is what you call assault and robbery I will do something for the next one.'

On the morning of the hearing, Dr Stonham picked out the two men from a police line up. In the courtroom Dr Stonham stated that he recognized the prisoners in the dock as two of the men who had taken part in the affair. Dr Stonham stated that Marsh held his arm and he believed that the other man, Thompson, was the man who had taken his watch. Edward Vickers, living at 5 Vine Court, gave evidence that he saw the doctor visit his patient and while the doctor was in the house, Thompson spoke to him and Marsh was present at the time. Mr Vickers said he later saw the doctor leave his patient's house and Marsh and Thompson forced him against a wall, assisted by three other men, although he could not see what they did to Dr Stonham. At the same time he heard some women scream for the doctor's life to be saved.

The doctor stated that his property had not been recovered and, since the attack, he had suffered considerably from shock. Mr Cluer, having heard that Thompson and Marsh had been previously convicted, said those convictions must be proved before him on Friday, at Worship Street, but the prisoners would now be bound over to give evidence at the trial, which would take place at the Old Bailey.

CHAPTER 13

Whitechapel Ruffians Find their Match
1897

*In the course of the struggle, Downes repeatedly hit
Miss Toffler in the face.*

n the front cover of *The Illustrated Police News*, on
Saturday, 6 November 1897, an illustration of a young
woman fighting with two men, caused much public mirth.

*Annie Toffler defends
herself valiantly, as she
is attacked by William
Downes and James
Cronin.* The Illustrated
Police News

Annie Toffler was set upon in broad daylight, by two ruffians intent on robbing her, in Cable Street, Whitechapel, but the two assailants got more than they bargained for. As one of them, William Downes, snatched the purse she was carrying, she took hold of him by the collar until he gave it back.

In the course of the struggle, Downes repeatedly hit Miss Toffler in the face. His companion, James Cronin, joined in the fighting and Annie defended herself valiantly. Cronin along with some of their associates, who had appeared on the scene, eventually forced her to release her hold on Downes. Fortunately, the police were able to apprehend the two villains, who were tried at the Old Bailey and found guilty of robbing the young woman. They were each sentenced to twelve months hard labour and to twelve strokes of the 'cat of nine tails'. Annie Toffler was commended for her courageous conduct and given a reward of £1.

An eighteenth century engraving of the Sessions House, precursor of the Old Bailey and Central Criminal Court. Trials were held in the open air to prevent disease spreading from the pestilence ridden criminals to the judge, lawyers and court officials. The bench and bail dock can be seen in the centre foreground. Author's collection

CHAPTER 14

Suicides
1899 & 1903

... he received a letter from his sweetheart, and in the afternoon he went to buy a revolver.

(1) A Publican's Worry Ends in Suicide, 1899

On Saturday, 1 July 1899 *The Illustrated London News* reported details of an inquest held at Poplar by Coroner Mr Wynne Baxter, on the body of a young man named Daniel Bowers, aged twenty-five years. The deceased was manager of the *Foresters Arms*, St Leonard's Road, Poplar. He was found dead in his bedroom on 18 June, with a bullet wound in his head. Mr Bowers was engaged to a barmaid, Miss Alice Carter, who worked at the *Liverpool Arms,* Canning Town. Their engagement had taken a place over a year before and they were to have been married in September. Witnesses stated that the dead man had recently appeared to be very strange in his manner. On the morning of the day he died, Monday, 18 July, he received a letter from his sweetheart, and in the afternoon he went to buy a revolver. He was afterwards found lying dead on his bedroom floor, with a bullet-wound in his mouth, and a five-chambered revolver, with one chamber empty, lying by his side. Miss Carter stated that she knew her fiancé had been upset about business matters. She told the court that she also remembered that about three months previously, when they were discussing his business affairs, he said that he would poison himself. At the time of his death, Daniel Bowers had £12 in gold in his possession. The jury returned a verdict of 'Suicide during temporary insanity.'

(2) Grieving Cabman Hangs Himself, 1899

… two years previously he had tried to commit suicide by cutting his throat with a razor.

In November 1899 an inquest was held at the Whitechapel Coroner's Court, before deputy coroner Dr E King Houshin, concerning the death of William Richardson, aged fifty-nine, a cabman, of 28 Mount Street, Whitechapel.

A witness, Mrs Elizabeth Smith of 29 Brown's Road, Plaistow, said that Mr Richardson had been suffering from failing sight for several years, which resulted in him being unable to get work. His wife had kept the home going but she had died the previous July, since when Richardson had become very depressed and had threatened to commit suicide.

Mrs Julia Garrett, of 28 Mount Street, the wife of a salesman, said that on Tuesday, 14 November, while standing at her room window she heard a noise, and saw Mr Richardson fall from the third floor window. At first she thought he had fallen while window cleaning, but afterwards found that he had thrown himself out and was hanging by a rope.

In his evidence, Police Constable John Elliott stated that the deceased had tied the rope round the bedstead and given himself a ten-foot drop. He added that Mr Richardson was quite dead when he body was dragged into the second floor window.

Other evidence showed that Mr Richardson's inability to find work due to his failing eyesight, preyed on his mind, and two years previously he had tried to commit suicide by cutting his throat with a razor. The jury returned a verdict of suicide while of unsound mind.

(3) Terrible Assault on Wife and Suicide of Husband, 1903
'Father has cut his throat!'

The Lout family lived at 230 Jubilee Street, Stepney. The head of the household, Jacob William Lout, was a shoemaker, and was fond of strong drink. In recent weeks he had been drinking more heavily than usual and those who knew him well noticed a change in his manner, which some described as strange. One morning, in August 1903, Mrs Lout was awakened by her drunken husband, who began striking her with a sash weight and a chopper. Mrs Lout's screams were heard by her daughter, who immediately came to her rescue and carried her into another room. Her daughter left the room and shortly afterwards Mrs Lout heard her call out 'Father has cut his throat.' Both Mr and Mrs Lout were conveyed to the hospital, where Mrs Lout received treatment for multiple injuries and shock. Mr Lout had three cuts to his throat and died of double-pneumonia, which resulted from his self-inflicted injuries. At the inquest held on 13 August, the jury returned a verdict of suicide while of unsound mind.

On Saturday 15 August 1903, The Illustrated Police News *reported a ferocious attack on a sleeping woman by her husband. Main Picture: Jacob Lout attacking his wife with a sash window weight.* **Top right:** *Mrs Lout is carried out of the bedroom by her daughter.* **Bottom right:** *Jacob Lout uses his razor to cut his throat.* The Illustrated Police News

(4) Sad Suicide of a Youthful Husband, 1899

When he saw the blood running down Maggie's face, he exclaimed, 'Oh, Maggie, I have done it!'

Walter Sidney Thurston, aged twenty-one, had married his wife, Margaret, at Christ Church, Spitalfields, during Easter 1898, whereupon they began their married life at their rented home at 1, Chapel Street, Spitalfields. Walter had great difficulty finding work, although he made every effort to do so. His main source of income was spasmodic and came from selling newspapers. He became very depressed at his lack of success and had threatened suicide.

HE HANGS HIMSELF ON THE CUPBOARD DOOR

AN EIGHTEEN-YEAR-OLD HUSBAND ATTACKS HIS WIFE.
HE THINKS HE HAS KILLED HER, AND COMMITS SUICIDE.

Main Picture: *Walter Thurston attacks his wife, Maggie, with a poker, as her father intervenes.*
Top left: *Maggie Thurston discovers her dead husband hanging from the cupboard door.*
The Illustrated Police News

On Tuesday, 21 January, Walter left early in the morning hoping to find work. He returned after only half-an hour and told his wife, who was in the kitchen talking to her father, that the landlord had given them notice to quit, as the rent had not been paid for two weeks. He then began to argue with Maggie, who was holding their one-month old baby in her arms, and within a few moments, he had become so irate that Maggie found herself being attacked by her husband, who had picked up a poker. Maggie's father intervened as Walter raised the poker to strike her, preventing the poker hitting its target. Walter dropped the poker and picked up a cup, which he flung across the room striking his wife on the head. When he saw the blood running down Maggie's face, he exclaimed, 'Oh, Maggie, I have done it!' He then ran out of the kitchen in a distraught state, apparently thinking he has killed her, and locked himself in the front room. After Maggie had washed her face and put the baby down to sleep, Maggie and her father tried to coax Walter out of the room for some time and eventually, after they could get no response, they broke down the door. When they entered he room, much to their dismay, they discovered that Walter had hanged himself. He was hanging from a rope he had suspended from the back of a cupboard door. He was already dead.

It was not until after her husband's death that Maggie Thurston discovered that he was not twenty-two years of age, as she believed him to be, but was only eighteen and he had been just seventeen at the time of their marriage. Walter's mother, Esther Parsons, wife of a commissionaire, identified him at the mortuary. He was the son of her first marriage. At the inquest Mrs Parsons said that she had no idea that her son was even married, until after she heard of his death. He had regularly visited herself and her husband and since he had been out of work had spent every Sunday with them.

Maggie Thurston appeared at her husband's inquest with her head bandaged. The Coroner commented that it appeared that Walter Thurston had been leading a double life. Maggie's father said that he knew nothing of his son-in-law until after the marriage. He also commented that it was extraordinary that two children could go and get married without their parents knowing anything about it. The jury returned a verdict of suicide while of unsound mind.

CHAPTER 15

A Mad Cow's Antics Bring Memories of Foul Deeds Flooding Back
1899

... there was a whole series of attacks on members of the public, by criminals using cattle as a means of robbing unsuspecting members of the public.

An article that appeared in *The Illustrated Police News*, on Saturday, 15 April 1899, concerning stampeding cattle brought memories of more sinister events flooding back to some of the East End's more elderly residents. It was reported that:

About half-past eight on Saturday night [8 April 1899] *three cows were detrained at Liverpool Street goods station from a farm close to Enfield, and, in charge of three drovers, proceeded by way of Middlesex Street to their destination, the yard of a Mr Lambert, a dairyman in Fairclough Street, Commercial Road. One had just lost her calf, and owing to the turmoil and excitement of the streets became excited. Beginning to rush wildly about she darted down Stoney Lane, knocking down Morey Marks, a boy of nine years, and scattering his companions in all directions. Here she was headed back into Middlesex Street, and rushed along the whole length of the street, while the screaming of the women and children only helped to madden the, now infuriated, beast. Crossing the traffic in Aldgate, she rushed up Arrow Alley. Here, all unaware of what was coming, was Herman Geeling, forty-four, a waiter, of 2, Chickwell Hill, St. George's, who was coming into Aldgate to make a few purchases. The cow, rushing blindly on, pinned the man in a corner, and lowering her head, plunged her horns into the unfortunate man's abdomen, ripping him up for about ten inches. He was picked up as soon as the beast freed herself , and taken to the London Hospital…in spite of attempts to lasso her, the cow next plunged through the door of a dairy in Mansell Street, kept by a Mr Foulkes, smashing everything in its path, and upsetting a large quantity of milk … the animal turned round and rushed back into Arrow Alley, where it wedged itself between a wall and a post at the corner of a narrow piece of pavement opposite the Green Man and Still. Then some strong ropes were procured, and the animal's head tied to the post while a conveyance was sent for...The infuriated beast was eventually got into a cart, and driven to Commercial Road.*

On hearing about this incident, the East End's oldest residents cast their minds back to events that occurred earlier in the century. On Lady Day in 1818, a crowd consisting of several hundred men seized a bullock and used it as a battering ram, when they attacked a silk warehouse. The staff at the warehouse were obliged to defend themselves and did so by firstly pouring boiling water on their attackers from above. After shotguns were discharged from within the

Herman Geeling is gored by a rampaging cow in Arrow Alley, on 8 April 1899. The Illustrated Police News

warehouse, the terrified bullock ran amok and tossed and injured some of the crowd, before falling down dead, presumably from fright.

At that time and well into the twentieth century, cattle, were not an uncommon sight in the streets of the East End and the poor beasts were often used for nefarious purposes. Eight years after the silk warehouse incident, in 1826, there was a whole series of attacks on members of the public, by criminals using cattle as a means of robbing unsuspecting members of the public. As the twilight hours turned to darkness, gangs would drive terrified cattle through the streets and by some means cause them to stampede and charge down anyone who got in their way. Those who fell were robbed as they lay on the ground.

One of Doré's mid-Victorian views of Blue Gate Fields, Shadwell. Author's collection

CHAPTER 16

Edgar Edwards and the Murder of the Darby Family
1902

Detective Sergeant Friend, in his evidence at Stratford Police Court said, he was present when the bodies were exhumed and described the contents of the six sacks in which the dissected bodies were found.

On the late afternoon of Tuesday, 23 December 1902, sinister events at a house in Leyton attracted the attention of passers by. The sound of breaking glass, loud banging and cries for help was noticed by several people, including the driver of a tram and his conductor. Robert Smith and Herbert Pitt, realising that something serious was amiss, left their tram car and went to investigate. They were joined by a dustman, George Wheatley, who had been summoned by a startled little girl. As they approached 89 Church Road, the front door of the house burst open and an elderly man staggered out with blood pouring from his head. The injured man was followed by another man, who, upon seeing the men approaching the house, fled from the scene. George Wheatley followed the fleeing man as he ran around the back of the group of houses known as Worcester Villas. There he saw the man washing his blood soaked hands in an old bathtub. On being confronted by Wheatley, the man climbed over garden fences before he retreated into the back door of No 89.

PC Matthews, who was patrolling his beat was quickly on the scene. When he arrived, the elderly man was sitting in a dazed condition on the pavement being attended to by other passers by. Leaving the front door guarded, Constable Matthews, accompanied by Robert Smith, went through the neighbouring house, No 91, to the back garden. They climbed the fence into the garden of No 89 and entered the house through the back door. On discovering nobody on the ground floor, they went upstairs where they found the door to one room locked from the inside and were obliged to force the door to gain admittance. When they entered the room a man was sitting on a bed, changing his blood soaked shirt. When Constable Matthews said that he would be arrested, the man accused the elderly gentleman of having assaulted him first. The man was taken to Stratford Police Station, where he gave his name as Edgar Edwards and his occupation as grocer's clerk. He was formally charged with assault whereupon Edwards replied, 'I am very sorry it occurred. We had been drinking together.' Meanwhile, the injured man, one John Garland, was taken to West Ham Hospital, where he was detained for a week with head injuries.

When the police investigation into events began, the stories told by the two men differed considerably. According to Edwards, he and Garland had been drinking together in the nearby *Oliver Twist* public house. He intimated that, possibly as a result of the alcohol they had consumed, an argument ensued and Garland became violent and attacked him. Edwards said he had simply defended himself. Once Mr Garland had sufficiently recovered to be able to talk to the police, he told an entirely different story.

Mr and Mrs John Garland ran a grocery business in Godrell Road, Victoria Park. They decided to sell the business and approached Duggan & Co. of Bishopsgate to act as their agents. The business was advertised for sale at £80. On 18 December, Edwards arrived at Garland's shop with an order to view. Edwards expressed an interest in buying the business. It being too late in the day to go to Duggan & Co. to finalise matters, Edwards said he would write to arrange an appointment.

On 22 December Mr Garland received a letter from Edgar Edwards. It read:

> *As I shall be at Leyton tomorrow, could you make it convenient to meet me at eleven o'clock at 89 Church Road, Leyton to talk over matters, and accompany me to Duggans in order to make the necessary arrangements and pay a substantial deposit.*

The letter arrived at Mr Garland's address after the time of Edwards' suggested meeting. So, Mr Garland went to Bishopsgate to consult his agents, then sent a telegram to the address on Edwards' letter, 5 Barnsbury Road, Islington, informing him that his letter had arrived too late for him to attend his proposed meeting. On Tuesday, 23 December, Mr Garland received another letter from Edwards, informing him:

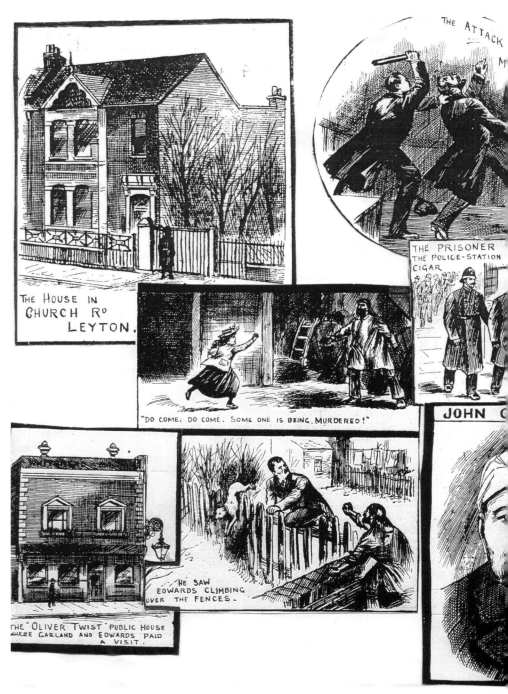

A series of drawings showing the events at 89 Church Road on Tuesday, 23 December 1902 and the immediate aftermath. The Illustrated Police News

SCENE OUTSIDE. THE POLICE COURT STRATFORD.

SASH WEIGHT FOUND BY THE POLICE

HAT WORN BY MR GARLAND. WHEN HE. WAS ATTACKED

WILLIAM JONES

THE MAN WHO BOUGHT THE SASH-WEIGHT

THE PRISONER.

Waited about at Leyton until past one o'clock. Saw nothing of you. Must be there again tomorrow and if you can possibly make it convenient to see me at 89 Church Road between eleven and twelve, I should be greatly obliged. The facts are these. I have just let the house, and the tenant wants to come in on Wednesday and there are some repairs that require my superintendence. Hoping you can see me there tomorrow, as I have so much on my hands just now.

The following morning Mr Garland set of for Leyton and arrived in Church Road at about eleven o'clock. He was invited into No 89 by Edwards, and when he entered the house he noticed that the ground floor was completely empty. Edwards told him that he was waiting for a carpenter to arrive but he was doing some work on another of his properties in Clapton and would probably not come for another hour or so. Having discussed various matters pertaining to the grocery business in Victoria Park, Edwards suggested that they should adjourn to the *Oliver Twist*, and go to Duggan and Co. to pay a deposit, once he

The Oliver Twist, *where Edgar Edwards drank with John Garland, seen here in November 2004. In recent years, this pub has become well-known to television viewers, through the popular series* London's Burning, *in which it has been featured in many episodes.* John D Murray

had given his instructions to the carpenter. They each had two glasses of ale, then returned to Worcester Villas. They waited a while longer at the house, before going back to the *Oliver Twist*, where they remained until about three o'clock, then returned once again to the house.

Mr Garland was anxious to conclude matters, and pointed out to Edwards, that his wife was alone, as there was nobody else at all employed in the shop. This fact seemed to interest Edwards greatly. Having waited a while longer, Mr Garland said that it would be too late to go to Bishopsgate to Duggan & Co. and decided to return home. Edwards produced a piece of paper and said he would leave a note for the carpenter and go with him. Edwards had been carrying what Mr Garland assumed to be plans of the house in his right hand. As Mr Garland walked down the dark passageway to the front door, Edwards struck him on the head with the roll of 'papers'. Taken totally by surprise Mr Garland fell to the floor with Edwards continuing to strike him on the head as he was falling. Mr Garland, his head now bleeding profusely, desperately tried to defend himself and summoned from within the strength to struggle to his feet, whilst Edwards continued with the attack. Mr Garland called out 'Don't murder me – what have I done?' Edwards tried to stifle Mr Garland's cries for help but Mr Garland managed to break a pane of glass in the street door and his calls for help and the ensuing noise was heard. The door burst open and Mr Garland escaped from the house, as three men were approaching it.

Once the police had taken statements from both men they continued with their investigations. According to Edwards he was attacked first but Garland insisted that Edwards had attempted to kill him, and that the attack was completely unprovoked.

Detective Inspector Collins and Inspector Young went to 89 Church Road to see the crime scene themselves. In the passageway leading to the front door there were bloodstains on the floor and ceiling. There were also bloodstains on the scullery door and window. On the floor were a five-pound sash window weight and a roll of paper, the evidence suggested that the sash weight had been concealed in the roll of paper, as the weight was covered with blood and hair. Upstairs in the back bedroom, they found a bloodstained shirt and vest. They also found various items of women's clothing, several pawn tickets and some business cards bearing the name W J Darby, 22 Wyndham Road, Camberwell.

Not unlike today, in 1902, Church Road, Leyton was a long, winding road, leading from High Road, Leyton, to the Lea Bridge

Road. The house that became the focus of a murder investigation has been pulled down, but in 1902, 89 Church Road was one of three red-brick houses known as 'Worcester Villas' that closely adjoined Leyton Cricket Ground. The house had extensive views over fields, both to the back and to the front. It was a two-storeyed house, with an ornamental stone front, whose ground floor comprised a parlour, kitchen and scullery. Upstairs there were three bedrooms. At the back of the house was a garden, oblong in shape and about seventy feet long. The rent for the property was ten shillings a week. The landlord was auctioneer and estate agent, Mr W J Bassett, of Lorne Terrace, Lea Bridge Road. He said that, in response to his request, Edwards sent him a letter of reference, purported to have been signed by W J Darby The reference proving satisfactory, Mr Bassett took a deposit from Edwards and the first weeks' rent. Edwards secured the services of a retired grave-digger, Joseph Rawlings, to dig the garden over. He lived nearby at 79 Church Road. In his evidence Rawlings stated that he was asked to 'get the job finished as soon as possible. I expect my wife and family here soon, and want the garden to look as neat as may be.' It was on Monday, 8 December, while Rawlings was at work on the garden that Edwards arrived at the house with a four-wheeled van, loaded up with an assortment of furniture, some heavy wooden boxes and a tin one. On Edward's instructions he carried various items up the stairs and into a bedroom.

After Edwards failed to pay Mr Bassett the rent for the second and third week of his tenancy, and on discovering that a charge of assault had been preferred against him, Mr Bassett decided to look further into his tenant's background. When he compared a letter written to him by Edwards, he noticed a striking resemblance to the handwriting of his letter of reference from Mr Darby. He decided to go to Camberwell to enquire after Mr Darby. When he arrived at Wyndham Road, he discovered that No 22 was a small grocery shop with living accommodation above, and that until recently it had been run by a young couple, Mr and Mrs William Darby, who had a baby daughter, and they had lived above the shop. He was also alarmed to discover that Mr Darby, his wife and child had mysteriously disappeared. Mr Bassett went back to Leyton and made this matter known to the police.

At the request of the police in Leyton, Detective Sergeant Melville was sent from Camberwell Police Station to 22 Wyndham Road, to make enquiries. When they visited the premises, they found it to be

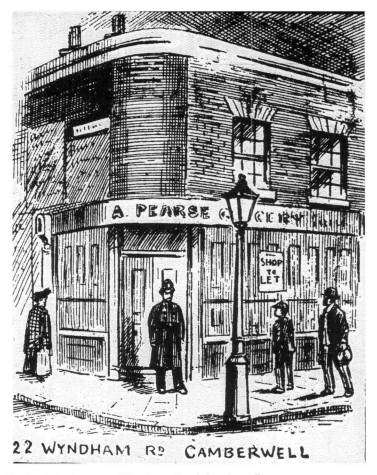

The Darby's shop at 22 Wyndham Road, Camberwell. The Illustrated Police News

a small shop situated at the end of a narrow thoroughfare known as Crown Street, having one window in Crown Street and the other in Wyndham Road, the front door being on the apex of the junction of the two streets. The shop, was now being managed by a four feet, ten inches tall, hunch-back, named Goodwin, and his wife, on behalf of Edgar Edwards. Further enquiries locally revealed the astonishment of many of the shop's customers at the apparently sudden disappearance of the Darbys without any plausible explanation. Some expressed concerns about the Christmas Club money paid to the Darbys, with which presents and comestibles were to be bought for the festive season. It transpired that about the beginning of

December Mrs Darby's sister, Mrs Alice Baldwin, received a letter from Mrs Darby, from the shop in Camberwell , asking her to come over and see her baby, which had been born on 28 September, as it was ill. Mrs Baldwin travelled from her home in Glenwood Road, Catford, to Camberwell but on entering the shop found a strange man behind the counter, who said he had bought the business. In response to inquiries he said that Mrs Darby might be in in a few minutes, and asked Mrs Baldwin to wait as the Darby's furniture was still there. He invited Mrs Baldwin inside the living quarters but in consequence of what she described as 'his piercing eyes,' she refused to do so.

Mrs Alice Baldwin, Mrs Darby's sister. The Illustrated Police News

Mrs Baldwin hung around the vicinity of the shop for about two hours, and questioned some of the neighbours as to whether they had seen Mrs Darby. Nobody had seen Mrs Darby or her husband since the man had taken possession of the shop.

The Darbys had kept a china shop in the High Road, Leytonstone, until about twelve months previously. They had then moved to Camberwell, where they took over a grocer's business at 22 Wyndham Road. Unfortunately the business failed to reach the Darby's expectations, so they put it up for sale and advertised in various newspapers on Friday, 7 November. The advertisement ran:

GROCERY, General and Provisions;
Genuine business for disposal; doing £ 8 to
£10 weekly, has done £18; price £60, all at,
or close after. – 22 Wyndham-road, Camberwell.

Among those showing and interest in the business was Edgar Edwards. After discussion, an arrangement was arrived at and Edwards took possession of the business on 1 December. After that date the movements of the Darbys are not known, as the neighbours had no definite recollection of seeing them again.

Edwards had approached the Goodwins on 28 November, at their home in Elsted Street, Walworth, and said he might have an opportunity for them. He had known Mr Goodwin for years as they

The Darby Family. The Illustrated Police News

had attended the same school together, Fellows Street School in Hackney Road. He said he needed someone who he could trust to manage the shop for him. He also asked Mr Goodwin if he could obtain a sash weight for him. He said it was to be used for opening and closing a shop door, at a shop he owned in Battersea. However, no shop belonginging to Edwards in Battersea was ever traced and probably never existed. He returned to the Goodwin's house on 30 November and discussed the management of his shop in Camberwell in detail. They were keen to take it on. They talked until late and Edwards stayed overnight. He departed the following morning, after breakfast, taking with him the sash weight that Mr Goodwin had obtained for him, after commenting that it would do very nicely. However, Mrs Goodwin was puzzled at Edward's apparent lack of money, as he asked her to pawn an umbrella for him. She did so and obtained one shilling and sixpence. Nobody reported having seen the Darby family following that fateful morning of Monday, 1 December.

Mr and Mrs Goodwin met Edwards later that morning and he took them to the shop a little after noon. However, after briefly showing them around, he suggested that they go and eat and return at 1.30 pm. It later emerged that, while the Goodwins went to get some food, Edwards went to a pawnbroker's and pawned John Darby's gold watch and chain for £7. He signed the contract note W T Lowden. The duplicate of this contract note was found at 89 Church Road, Leyton. When the Goodwins returned they found the shop was open for business and Edwards gave Mrs Goodwin thirty-two shillings, with which she redeemed his umbrella and also some clothes. The Goodwins never saw the living quarters above the shop. So far as they knew, Edwards slept on the premises, for he let them out every night and let them in every morning from December 2 to 10 inclusive. Edwards told Mr Goodwin that he was trading under the name of Lowdon and that William Darby sometimes came to see him at night. The Goodwins undertook to keep the shop open from 8 am to 10 pm for a wage of thirty shillings (£1.50p) a week.

On the evening of 1 December the landlord of 22 Wyndham Road, Mr John Knight, paid a call, expecting to see Mr Darby. He told Edwards that he had seen Mr Darby two days previously to discuss matters regarding the transfer of the tenancy in the event of him selling his business, and Mr Knight had been expecting another visit from him earlier that evening. Edwards told Mr Knight that he was aware of the matter but could give no explanation why Mr Darby had not kept his appointment. At the end of the first week, the takings being meagre, Edwards reduced the Goodwin's wages by ten shillings to £1. During this week, Edwards, through Mr Goodwin hired from a Mr Greenfield a light cart, which is supposed to have been used in conveying his goods to Leyton. He had the light cart with the pony twice, for about four hours each time, and a horse and van for a whole day. The pony he drove himself. The van, in which the Darby's furniture was taken away, he hired with a driver.

Mr Knight made several further visits to the shop and was most perturbed that he could not see Mr Darby. Edwards told him that he had now concluded matters regarding the purchase of the business and he was anxious that the tenancy should be transferred to him. However, Mr Knight had taken a dislike to Edwards and told him not to purchase any stock as he would not transfer the tenancy to him under any circumstances. The end of the matter came on 10 December when Mr Knight instructed bailiffs to enter the premises for non-payment of rent. However, Edwards had clearly foreseen this potential problem and had already taken steps to secure other premises. He made enquiries at several agents to see if there were any businesses for sale. At one he visited on 3 December, belonging to a Mr Hacker, he gave his name as William Darby. He eventually approached Mr Bassett, who had a house to rent at 89 Church Road, Leyton, and perhaps was attracted by the large garden. Having secured the tenancy, Edwards arrived at the house at 11'oclock on the night of Friday, 5 December, in what one witness described as some sort of butcher's cart, having obtained the keys to the house from a neighbour, Mr Childs. Mr Childs worked as a milkman, and he was most displeased at being disturbed so late in the evening, considering his early rising occupation.

Edwards made two visits to the house on Monday, 8 December, when he drove a pony and cart. A four-wheeled van delivered more of his belongings later. The police believed that the wooden boxes and tin trunk removed from the Wyndham Road shop and taken to 89 Church, Road, Leyton, in the four-wheeled van, and unloaded by Joseph Rawlings, contained the remains of the Darby family.

It is clear that Edwards continued to search for other suitable businesses. On 19 December, Edwards, calling himself William Darby, visited the Theobolds Road offices of estate-agent Charles W West. On the same day, Frank Dale, a grocer, of Havant Road, Walthamstow, who had placed his business for disposal, received a visit from Edwards. He expressed an interest and promised to come again but never reappeared. Edwards also approached another grocer, Ernest Holt, of Dalston Lane, Hackney. It seems likely that Edwards was lining up several possible targets in his bizarre efforts to secure a chain of grocery stores, at little or no cost to himself.

On 9 December Edwards was in Whitechapel Road when he saw an acquaintance of his, a man he had known for over fifteen years, and to whom he was known as Edgar Owen. William Jones, was a painter who lived in nearby Commercial Street. Edwards asked him if he could obtain a five-pound sash weight for him, for which he gave him a shilling. Having purchased the sash weight, Mr Jones accompanied Edwards to Leyton, where he did various small jobs at 89 Church Road, including cleaning the windows. But he found all the window sashes to be working perfectly.

A series of drawings showing the discovery of the remains of the Darby family, the hearing in Stratford Police Court, with Mr Garland in the witness box, and the various people associated with events at the house in Leyton. The Illustrated Police News

TTHEWS

OR YOUNG .

POLICE OFFICIALS EXAMINE THE VAN

FINDING THE REMAINS OF THE DARBY FAMILY IN THE BACK GARDEN. CHURCH RD LEYTON

J . G

Edwards first appeared at Stratford Police Court on 24 December, the day after his attack on John Garland. His manner throughout was arrogant. At a hearing on 27 December, Edwards gave the impression that he was more concerned as to the whereabouts of his gold-rimmed spectacles, which had been taken from him, than he was about anything he might be accused of. He complained about being deprived of his spectacles and referred to his mistreatment by Inspector Young:

> *You gave me permission to retain them on the last occasion – no, no, December 24 – But since then in defiance of that order, the police have deprived me of them in a brutal manner. This officer, Inspector Young, he is about the greatest brute I ever met …*

Following John Garland's statement that Edward's attack on him had been completely unprovoked, combined with the unexplained disappearance of the Darby family, the police were growing increasingly suspicious that something untoward had happened to the Darbys and suspected that Edwards might be involved. They asked Mrs Darby's sister, Mrs Alice Baldwin, to accompany them to the house in Church Road, Leyton. Once there, she was taken to the upstairs back bedroom, where she identified various items of clothing belonging to her sister, including her wedding dress. Mrs Baldwin expressed her amazement that her sister's only winter coat was there. How could she have gone without that? The police then turned their attention to the newly dug garden.

Not long after Edwards had moved into 89 Church Road and after Joseph Rawlings had dug the garden over and cleared the rubbish away, a neighbour, Mrs Sophia Frear, saw Edwards digging a deep hole. She knew it was deep because he was standing in it and she could just see the top of his head. The following day she noticed that the hole had been filled in and the ground levelled. When the police arrived on the morning of Tuesday, 30 December, to begin their search of the garden, DS Melville, DS Friend and PC Hughes, were faced with considerable difficulty. Because the entire garden had been completely transformed by Mr Rawlings' efforts, it was impossible to distinguish where any evidence might have been buried. Edwards' additional digging could not at first be detected. However, they eventually came across an area where there were signs that the deeper soil had recently been disturbed. They continued to dig deeper and wider. At noon, at a depth of over five feet, a gruesome discovery was made. In six sacks were the remains of Mr and Mrs Darby and their baby daughter.

The Darbys had a pet dog, a Manchester terrier. That dog was at Edwards' house in Leyton. Neighbours later reported that the dog was often seen to run to a spot in the garden, looked puzzled, then lie down on the newly dug earth. There the remains of his master and mistress were found.

Detective Sergeant Friend, in his evidence at Stratford Police Court said, he was present when the bodies were exhumed and described the contents of the six sacks in which the dissected bodies were found. He said that he showed a number of articles of clothing found to Mrs Baldwin – Mrs Darby's sister. He discovered in one sack a solitaire shirt stud, the counterpart of which was found on the dressing table at 89 Church Road.

A post-mortem examination of the remains was conducted by Dr Jekyll, the divisional police surgeon, Dr Sandilands and Dr Dawson (who was attending John Garland at West Ham Hospital). They concluded that the position and nature of the wounds suggested that the crime was deliberately planned and carried out with methodical precision. Mr and Mrs Darby had received crushing blows on the skull. The baby had a wound over the eye, insufficient in itself to cause death but certainly the blow that inflicted it would have caused unconsciousness.

On Thursday, 31 December at Stratford Police Court Edgar Edwards was charged as follows:

Edgar Edwards, you are charged on remand with unlawfully and maliciously wounding John Garland by striking him on the head with a piece of iron and inflicting grievous bodily harm upon him on December 23.

Then, much to Edwards' astonishment the charges against him continued:

You are further charged with feloniously killing and slaying William John Darby, aged twenty-six, Beatrice Darby, his wife, aged twenty-eight, and Eleanor Beatrice Darby, aged three months, on or about November 26, it is supposed at 22, Wyndham Road, Camberwell.

The *Evening News* reported:

Edwards is described by one who saw him at the police court as a man about thirty-four years of age, of a sullen and determined expression, not above the average height and of dark complexion. He speaks with a strong Scotch accent.

Following the coroner's inquest held at Leyton Town Hall and the hearings held at Stratford Police Court, a further hearing followed in Lambeth. On Saturday, 31 January, 1903 *The Illustrated London News* reported:

The 'Woman in Black' Appears in Court and Tells Her Story.
The latest striking features in the case against Edgar Edwards, at Lambeth Police Court, who is charged with the murder of Mr and Mrs William Darby, and their child, were the production of the sash weight found in the Camberwell house and the appearance of the "woman in black." The weight was exhibited by Sergeant Melville, of the Leyton police, who pointed out blood stains, and said that hair was clinging to it when discovered in a back room at 22, Wyndham Road. Sarah Summers, around whom a certain mystery has hung had comparatively little to tell …

Lambeth Police Court, where a further hearing was heard. The Illustrated Police News

Sarah Summers, the mysterious 'woman in black', was described in various contemporary accounts as being middle-aged. During the course of investigations it transpired that she had known Edwards for several years, and thirteen years before the events in Leyton had had a child by him. Although Edwards had not been in touch with her for several years, he called on her at her Hampstead home on Wednesday, 26 November 1902, with an attractive proposition. He told her that he was now in a position to provide a home for her, as he had just bought a shop with living accommodation, which was fully furnished. He also told her the previous owner had died. He suggested that as well as living on the premises, she should look after the shop for him. He called to see he again on the morning of the 28th and suggested that he take her to view the premises that evening. However, Edwards did not follow up his offer but simply sent a telegram stating that he had changed his mind. The next Sarah Summers heard of him was in the aftermath of the discovery of the remains in Church Road, Leyton.

On Wednesday, 4th February the *Evening News* reported:

> *At Lambeth Police Court today – when asked if he had anything to say, Edwards in a firm voice replied, 'Your worship, I wish to reserve my defence till the trial, and I plead not guilty.' He was then committed for trial at the Old Bailey Sessions, which begin next week.*

Edwards' trial was held in the Central Criminal Court at the Old Bailey before Mr Justice Wright, and began on Thursday, 12 February. Mr R D Muir and Mr Arthur Gill conducted the prosecution for the Crown. Mr Percival Hughes and Mr Paul Methuen acted for the defence. Edward's arrogance remained with him to the last, as the following exchange shows:

Mr Justice Wright: *Do you plead Guilty or Not Guilty?*

Edwards stood defiant and made no reply.

Mr Justice Wright: *Are you Guilty or Not Guilty?*
Edgar Edwards: *You have no business to ask me such a question.*
Mr Justice Wright: *You must answer Yes or No.*
Edgar Edwards: *Stuff and nonsense.*

Unable to extract a plea from Edwards, Mr Justice Wright directed that a plea of Not Guilty be recorded. The prosecution case presented overwhelming evidence against Edwards. On the opening day of the trial Mr Muir detailed the facts for the prosecution. When he had spoken for half an hour, Edwards, in an irritated manner, called out, 'Hurry up, chappie, and let's get through.'

When Mr Hughes, counsel for defence, rose to address the court, his only course of action was to suggest that his client was of unsound mind. Edwards' defence presented just one witness and requested that this witness should be able to give his evidence with only the judge knowing his true identity. Mr Hughes addressed the packed court, explaining his unusual request:

The reason is that the witness, who is an uncle of the prisoner by marriage and is in a good position in life, has three daughters. One of them is a resident in an asylum and the two others are in such a precarious condition mentally that he believes that if it came to their knowledge that they are related to the prisoner it might lead to their losing the balance of their minds.

This request was denied but Mr Justice Wright said that although in ruling he could not comply with counsel's request for secrecy, he had no doubt that the gentlemen of the press would withhold the witness's name from their publications. The gentlemen of the press duly obliged. However, there were no great revelations made by this witness. Other than stating the Edgar Edwards' real name was Edwin Owen and that several of his relatives were of unsound mind, little else was of any relevance. It also emerged during the trial that the prisoner's uncle died in an asylum, that the prisoner's grandfather's sister was also in an asylum and that his father died a complete dipsomaniac, after squandering the fortunes of his wife, two sisters and mother.

In his summing-up on behalf of the defence, Mr Hughes played on his claim that Edwards was insane:

… the prisoner was insane at the time he committed the act and was, therefore, not responsible for his actions. It is my contention that the crime was committed under an uncontrollable impulse…The enormity of the crime placed it beyond the possibility of being one which could be committed by a sane man. The conception and execution of the plan indicated that it could only have been done by a man incapable of controlling himself.

In his summing up, the judge, Mr Justice Wright stated:

> *The law is that, for the purpose of criminal trials, it must be shown on behalf of a prisoner that he suffered from disease or disorder of the mind which disabled him at the time he committed the crime from understanding the nature and character of the act he was doing. If he understood the nature and character of the act, the law said he was guilty. It was for the Crown to pardon or to commute a sentence if there was any reason for so doing. Was there any ground on which the jury could rightly and truly say that the prisoner was insane?... Mere soundness of mind was not enough. If that were to be recognized as a ground on which juries could act I do not know what would happen to society. If it were to be held that because a crime was ferocious, therefore the person who committed it must be insane, it would be holding out a direct incentive to people who committed crimes to make them ferocious in order that they might be excused on the grounds of insanity.*

Dealing with the facts, Mr Justice Wright said, it was a question for the jury whether, on the evidence, they could find that the prisoner was insane at the time he committed the act. It was his duty, however, to tell them that there was no trace of that kind of insanity in this case to justify the view that the prisoner was insane.

The jury retired at five minutes to twelve on Friday, 20 February, to consider their verdict. Edwards was taken to the cells below in charge of five warders. The jury, after a deliberation of half an hour, returned into the court, and the prisoner was brought into the dock. Nobody in that crowded courtroom seemed surprised when the foreman of the jury announced that they found the prisoner Guilty. When the Clerk of Arraigns asked the prisoner 'Have you anything to say why sentence of death should not be passed upon you according to law?' he replied, 'No. Get on with it. Get it over quickly. Get them along.' As the judge donned the customary black cap before pronouncing the death sentence, Edwards (who was closely surrounded by warders) called out from the dock, 'This is like being on the stage.' The 'drama' continued:

> **Mr Justice Wright:** *Edgar Edwards, the jury have found the only verdict possible according to their oaths and consciences. After a long career of crime, in which you have received sentences amounting to some fifteen years' penal servitude, you have been found guilty of committing a most terrible murder.*

The series of events at Camberwell and Leyton as recounted at the Old Bailey The Illustrated Police News

POLICE NEWS.
February 21, 1903.

EDWARDS LAUGHING

RDS ... SES TROUBLE AT ...KTON PRISIN

PRISONER TAKING NOTES

THE BLACK CAP

MR MUIR K.C

MR JUSTICE WRIGHT

EDWARDS REPEATEDLY ASKED FOR WATER

EDWARDS LISTENING TO THE DEATH SENTENCE

INCIDENTS IN THE TRIAL

ERER CONDEMNED TO DEATH.

Edgar Edwards: *I wish, my lord, you would pass sentence upon me as quickly as possible.*
Mr Justice Wright: *I have only now to pass the sentence of the law upon you. It is that you be taken hence to the place from whence you came, and from thence to a lawful place of execution, and that there you be hanged by the neck until you are dead –*
Edgar Edwards: *Good, good.*
Mr Justice Wright: [continuing] *and that your body be buried within the precincts of the prison wherin you shall have been last confined after your conviction. And may the Lord have mercy on your soul.*

As these final word were being uttered, Edwards burst into a fit of laughter. The condemned man quickly descended the steps leading from the dock and after being detained for a short time in the temporary prison adjoining the Sessions House, where he was thoroughly searched, he was removed in the prison van to Wandsworth Prison. Edwards was said to have remarked as he was being driven away from the Old Bailey 'You'd better take good care of me. I'll get away if there's a ghost of a chance.'

Edward's period of detention in Brixton Gaol during his trial had proved an extremely irksome task to the officials. Their utmost vigilance had been required to prevent him cheating the hangman. Confined to a special observation cell, a warder was continually looking through spy holes to see that all was well. On the morning of Friday, 20 February, Edwards managed to create some confusion. When the warders went to remove him from his cell to the Old Bailey, it was discovered that by some ingenious method, Edwards had contrived to tamper with the lock. And the door to his cell, which opened outwards, could not be opened. The time for Edwards' appearance at the Central Criminal Court was fast approaching and the fear that both judge and jury would be kept waiting, urged the officials to break the door off its hinges, all the while his gaolers were being laughed at sneeringly and defiantly by the prisoner. Edwards was convicted of wilful murder that day and returned to Brixton for the night. The following morning, Saturday, 21 February, he was removed to Wandsworth Prison.

On Saturday, 21 February 1903, *The Illustrated Police News* reported:

… Edwards is being more closely guarded than any prisoner ever before confined in Wandsworth Gaol. Two warders are constantly in the

February 28, 1903.   **THE ILLUSTRATED POLICE NEWS.**   3

EDWARDS IN THE CONDEMNED CELL.

[SUBJECT OF ILLUSTRATION.]

EDGAR EDWARDS, the notorious murderer of the Darby family in the little shop at Wyndham Road, Camberwell, who was condemned to death at the Old Bailey, after a trial remarkable for the callousness and levity of the prisoner, now lies at Wandsworth Prison. The condemned cell in which the unhappy man must await the dawn of March 3, when the last dread penalty will be carried out, is a spacious apartment, rather comfortably furnished, the fixtures including a bedstead, a table, several chairs, and two warders, as well as Edwards himself. During the week some sensational stories have been related of the condemned murderer. It was said that inquire into the mental condition of Edwards have completed their report.

It has been forwarded to the Home Office, and, although not yet officially made public, it is understood that the medical men have not been able to discover anything that would justify the Home Secretary in advising His Majesty to respite the sentence of death.

The condemned man's behaviour changed considerably during the latter part of last week, and although he would not receive the ministrations of the prison chaplain, he has been very earnest in his talks with a Nonconformist minister whom he asked to visit him, and since Thursday last he has been to chapel service each morning, occupying the special pew set apart for condemned prisoners. Two warders sit each side of him during the service, and three others are outside should their services be required.

He has also been allowed to exercise for about half an hour each morning in the exercise shed since he has become quieter.

FEARFUL TRAGEDY AT HOVE.

Grocer's Manager Tries to Murder His Wife and then Commits Suicide.

A SHOCKING tragedy occurred at 59, Blatchington Road, a private house at the western end of an important business thoroughfare in Hove. Rayner Bell, a grocer's manager, aged thirty-three, attempted to murder his wife by cutting her throat with a razor, and then committed suicide. A neighbour, Mr. William Hackett, a relieving officer, was in his office next door when he heard screams proceeding from No. 59, and going outside heard children crying and a woman's voice calling "Help!" and "Joe." Just afterwards the street door was flung open, and a woman rushed forth in her night-clothes, exclaiming that she was going for a doctor. Mr. Hackett darted up the steps, and in at the moved to the Hove Dispensary, where she is progressing as favourably as can be expected. The body of the husband was removed to the mortuary to await an inquest.

It appears that Mr. Bell, who was of a quiet and retiring disposition, had been suffering from melancholia for some time past, and had been absent from business for a fortnight, during which time he consulted a specialist in London. Deceased, who is said to be a Norfolk man by birth, was formerly in London, but has been manager of the Home and Colonial Stores at Hove for five or six years.

THE GLASGOW FOOTBALL DISASTER.

AN official statement as to the Ibrox Football Disaster Fund states that 621 cases were dealt with. The vast majority of them have been settled on lines based on the Workmen's Compensation Act. The remaining cases are very serious, and do not admit of present settlement.

EDWARDS IN THE CONDEMNED CELL.

Edwards was giving the warders considerable trouble, and on three occasions the Governor, Major Knox, had been called to him. At times he feigned sleep, apparently to throw the warders off their guard, and possibly with the hope that he might be able to secure some weapon to overpower them while they believed him to be asleep. He displayed great violence in the cell, and, so one story had it, tried to smash his chair for no apparent reason. He used abominable language, and raved that no gallows should ever have his body. This is all untrue. Edwards is behaving himself fairly well, the only breaks being when he shows signs of great irritation, and paces up and down his cell from the window to the door.

The two specialists who were ordered to

A BOOK FOR LADIES.

The information contained in this book ought

Edwards has written a letter to one of his sisters begging forgiveness for the trouble and disgrace he has brought on the family. His mother, who is over eighty, and is living in a respectable part of North-East London, has been spared the knowledge of her son's position.

SUICIDE THROUGH A SLOT METER.

OLIVER ROGERS, seaman, adopted an extraordinary method of ending his life at Southampton.

He put three pennies into a slot gas-meter, and then fixed a long piece of india-rubber tubing to a burner. Turning on the gas, he placed over his head a pillow-slip, into which he put the end of the tube.

Then, lying on the bed, he allowed himself to be slowly suffocated.

He was dead when discovered. The fact open door, and burst into the back room on the ground floor, occupied by Mr. and Mrs. Bell.

A fearful sight met his gaze. Lying on the bed with his head hanging over the side was Mr. Bell, blood flowing freely from a gash in his throat. A glance showed that the man was beyond aid, and Mr. Hackett turned his attention to the woman, from a wound in whose throat blood was also streaming. While he was binding up the wound with a towel Mrs. Bell told him that she had been awakened by her husband attempting to cut her throat. She sprang out of bed and screamed for help, and then, having obtained a light, turned to the bed, where she saw her husband lying gasping with a blood-stained razor in his hand. She seized the weapon and flung it behind her into a corner of the room, where it was subsequently picked up by Mr. Hackett.

In the meantime Mrs. Murdoch, a relative of the Bells, who had fled down the street for the doctor, had brought back Dr.

A CREMATED TRAMP.

A Wanderer Falls Asleep in a Rick and is Partially Destroyed by Natural Heat.

ON the farm of a Mr. Hawkins, near Eccleshall, in Staffordshire, a labourer was cutting hay from a rick when he cut through the decomposed body of an elderly man and severed the head.

The hayrick was stacked last summer. The body is evidently that of a tramp, fifty or sixty years old, who probably fell asleep on the unfinished rick, and was covered up by the remainder of the harvest.

At the inquest the verdict was that the "unknown" was "found dead." Nothing but skin and bone remained of the body, the heat of the rick having partially effected cremation.

condemned cell, and three other warders patrol the corridor outside, ready to enter the cell at the first cry for assistance.

Edwards has maintained his sullen, vengeful manner. He spent the night at Brixton after his condemnation in cursing and raving. When received at Wandsworth on Saturday morning he refused absolutely to receive the chaplain or to listen to his prayers.

The task of guarding Edwards is a trying one. He cannot be punished for any of his actions in the cell, or pinioned down to prevent them. As a condemned man he has considerable latitude. He can see as many friends as he chooses and as often as he chooses, and he can order anything he likes to eat or drink. He is also allowed to have tobacco, but he did not ask for any luxuries on Sunday.

It was also reported in *The Illustrated Police News* on Saturday, 21 February 1903:

Edwards is said to have made a confession, which is in the hands of his solicitor. Madame Tussaud's have offered £200 for it, and another person has made an offer of £100 for the gold-rimmed pince-nez which he wore until deprived of them by the prison authorities.

On Friday, 27 February the London *Evening News* reported:

The Home Secretary decided this afternoon that the execution of Edgar Edwards for the murder of the Darby family at Camberwell must take place next Tuesday at Wandsworth Gaol.

On Saturday, 28 February 1903, an interesting account of Edwards in the condemned cell appeared in *The Illustrated Police News*:

EDGAR EDWARDS, the notorious murderer of the Darby family in the little shop of Wyndham Road, Camberwell, who was condemned to death at the Old Bailey, after a trial remarkable for the callousness and levity of the prisoner, now lies at Wandsworth Prison. The condemned cell in which the unhappy man must await the dawn of March 3, when the last dread penalty will be carried out, is a spacious apartment, rather comfortably furnished, the fixtures including a bedstead, a table, several chairs, and two warders, as well as Edwards himself. During the week some sensational stories have been related of the condemned murderer. It was said that Edwards was giving the warders considerable trouble, and on three occasions the Governor, Major Knox, had been called to him.

*At times he feigned sleep, apparently to throw the warders off their guard,
and possibly with the hope that he might be able to secure some weapon
to overpower them while they believed him to be asleep. He displayed
great violence in the cell, and, so, one story had it, tried to smash his chair
for no apparent reason. He used abominable language, and raved that
no gallows should ever have his body. This is all untrue. Edwards is
behaving himself fairly well, the only breaks being when he shows signs
of great irritation, and paces up and down his cell from the window to
the door.*

*The two specialists who were ordered to inquire into the mental
condition of Edwards have completed their report.*

*It has been forwarded to the Home Office, and although not yet
officially made public, it is understood that the medical men have not
been able to discover anything that would justify the Home Secretary in
advising His Majesty to respite the sentence of death.*

*The condemned man's behaviour changed considerably during the
latter part of last week, and although he would not receive the
ministrations of the prison chaplain, he has been very earnest in his talks
with a Noncomformist minister whom he asked to visit him, and since
Thursday last he has been to chapel service each morning, occupying the
special pew set apart for condemned prisoners. Two warders sit each side
of him during the service, and three others are outside should their
services be required.*

*He has also been allowed to exercise for about half an hour each
morning in the exercise shed since he has become quieter.*

*Edwards has written a letter to one of his sisters begging forgiveness for
the trouble and disgrace he has brought on the family. His mother, who
is over eighty, and is living in a respectable part of North-East London,
has been spared the knowledge of her son's position.*

The Execution of Edgar Edwards took place on the morning of
Tuesday, 3 March, 1903 at 9 am. That day the London *Evening News
And Evening Mail* reported:

*Within Wandsworth Gaol, at nine o'clock this morning, Edwin Owen,
otherwise Edgar Edwards, was hanged for the murder of the Darby
family ...*

*The execution was carried out under the supervision of Mr Under-Sheriff
Metcalfe by Billington and his assistant Pierrepont* [sic] *in the presence of
Major Knox, the governor of the prison, Dr Beamish, the medical
superintendent, the Rev. J.H. Phipps, the chaplain, and several warders.*

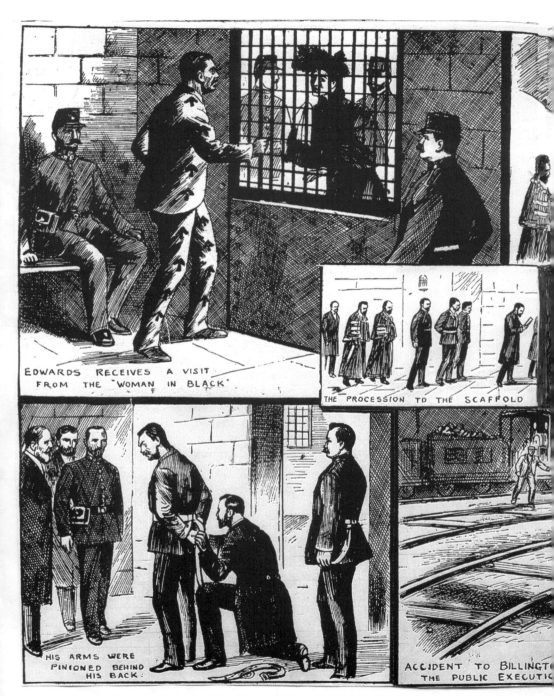

A series of drawings showing Edgar Edwards in the Condemned cell and the progress to his execution. Executioner Billington's mishap, following Edward's execution is also depicted.
The Illustrated Police News

BILLINGTON PULLED THE LEVER

THE PRISONER EDWARDS.

The execution shed is situated only fifty yards from the condemned cell, but is in the middle of the exercise yard, and there are several flower beds to make the yard like a pretty garden. All other prisoners were kept in their cells until noon.

The night before his execution, Edwards, showed a strong reluctance to go to bed, as required by prison regulation. Eventually, he did so and slept reasonably soundly, until he was aroused at 6 am, when he said to those attending him 'I'm ready. I shall give you no trouble.' At 7 am he ate a good breakfast, then asked to see the prison governor, whom he personally thanked for the kindness and indulgence allowed him. Edwards was attended my two Wesleyan chaplains in the condemned cell, who had given him the Lord's Supper in his cell the previous evening. At 7.45 am, a service was conducted in the condemned cell by the Reverend C H Kelly, assisted by the Reverend J Critchison, two warders were also present. Two more warders joined them in the cell later, but Edwards quietly submitted to the pinioning process. The prisoner was ghastly white as he was led to his execution. Both ministers accompanied Edwards (dressed in prison attire, as was the custom at that time) to the execution shed, the Reverend Kelly reading the last portion of the Burial Service on the scaffold. True to his word, Edwards gave no trouble. On his journey to the scaffold, he uttered several incoherent statements and also thanked the minister profusely for his administrations, making expressions of hope that God would forgive him for his misspent life. Edwards' last words to Reverend Kelly were 'I've been looking forward to this lot.' His last words distinguishable to those standing near were 'Good Lord, have mercy upon me.'

After the execution Reverend Kelly said that Edwards was quite repentant, and never asked for, expected, or desired a reprieve. Both Billington and Under-Sheriff Metcalfe described the execution officially as very easily carried out.

On Wednesday, 4 March 1903 the London *Evening News And Evening Mail* under the heading **BILLINGTON'S MISHAP Executioners Fall From a Midland Express Near Luton**, reported:

A peculiar incident happened at Luton early this morning to Billington, the executioner, who was travelling by the 12.15 a.m. express from St. Pancras to Bolton, after having executed Edwards…

One version of the affair is that the executioner fell out of the train. Another account represents that he was ejected from his compartment by some fellow passengers… Billington was found on the line [approaching Luton] after the train had passed, bruised and cut about the face and hands, but otherwise not seriously injured…Our correspondent says that Billington's explanation is that he had dozed off, and was awakened by rough handling from two or three men in the compartment with him, and that when he remonstrated with them he was pushed out

… Statement by the Police … About half a mile south from Luton a man was found lying in the permanent way. In answer to questions he gave his name as Billington, the public executioner, and his address as 96, Great Moor-street, Bolton… The doctor's examination showed that beyond a severe shaking, a sprained ankle, and a sprained left wrist the man had not sustained any very serious injuries.

Of Edgar Edward's situation, I will leave it to another murderer to have the final word. George Chapman (see Chapter 5), the notorious poisoner, believed by Chief Inspector Abberline to have been Jack the Ripper, and himself shortly to be executed, described Edwards as a 'hot 'un.' His description did not fall far short of the mark.

CHAPTER 17

Foul Murder in the *Lord Nelson,* Whitechapel

1903

Slowe hit Mary with his right fist and then with his left.

At about ten o'clock on Wednesday, 23 September 1903 a customer entered the public bar of the *Lord Nelson* at 299, Whitechapel Road and ordered a drink. He was served by twenty-year-old barmaid Mary Jane Hardwick., who had no liking for this occasional customer, and after serving him went to the private bar to avoid his company. The man's name was Charles Jeremiah Slowe, known to some simply as Jerry. Bystanders heard him ask Miss Hardwick if a certain man had been present earlier that day. That was the only conversation Slowe had with her that evening. He finished his drink and left. Shortly after midnight, when Miss Hardwick was engaged in turning out lights in preparation for closing, Slowe returned to the *Lord Nelson* and violently attacked her and stabbed her with a knife. Miss Hardwick died.

Mrs Jane Starkey, landlady of the *Lord Nelson* was Miss Hardwick's sister, Mrs Starkey's husband had died earlier that year on 11 March and she had decided to continue running the *Lord Nelson* herself. She said the murdered girl was an orphan and a native of Yeaden, near Leeds in Yorkshire. She was described as a girl of good appearance, had some musical accomplishments, was domesticated and ambitious. For several months she had assisted Mrs Starkey at the *Lord Nelson.*

Mrs Starkey said she knew Charles Slowe only as an occasional customer. Shortly after midnight she saw Slowe enter the front bar and at the time her sister, Mary, was looking out of the side door. He went up to her and struck her right and left. Mrs Starkey heard Slowe say, 'I've got you now,' and as she saw him hit her sister, Mrs Starkey screamed. She said Slowe hit Mary with his right fist and then with his left, but Mrs Starkey said she didn't see what he had in his hand as after hitting her, he kept the left hand down. Mrs Starkey didn't realise that he had stabbed her sister in the chest. As Mrs Starkey jumped over the bar to go to the assistance of her sister, Slowe ran out of the bar. Mrs Starkey followed him and called out to people in the street not to let him go. He was chased through several streets until he was caught and brought back into the *Lord Nelson* accompanied by a man named Pelling, who worked as a barman at the pub several other men who had joined in the chase, and a policeman. Meanwhile, Mrs Starkey had run back into the bar and found that her sister was swooning away.

Charles Ireland, a commission agent, of Brushfield Street, Bishopsgate, was in the *Hospital Tavern* and at 12.20 am. He heard screams from the *Lord Nelson,* which was opposite, and saw a man running down East Mount Street. He went across to the public bar of the *Lord Nelson,* where he saw Miss Hardwick lying across Mrs Starkey's knee.

The knife Slowe had used to stab Miss Hardwick was found lying on the pavement three or four yards from the door of the *Lord Nelson.* It was a broad-bladed dinner knife, with the blade narrowed for nearly the whole of its length, as if from long use and grinding.

When Slowe was brought out of the *Lord Nelson,* he remarked to the constable who took him in charge 'Catch hold of me tight, I have stabbed a woman.' However, Inspector Collins, who was in charge at Bethnal Green Police Station when Slowe was brought in, said the prisoner made no reply to the charge. Slowe gave his address as Rowton House, Whitechapel.

It transpired that, up until Christmas 1902, Mary Hardwick had been corresponding with a young man in her native Yeaden. The young man came to London on a visit and stayed for a few days at the *Lord Nelson* during which time he saw and spoke to Slowe several times. However, Miss Hardwick had ended her attachment to him after she had discovered that the young man had been seen walking out with another woman. As far as anyone knew there was no attachment between Miss Hardwick and Slowe. She did not like him and her lack of response to the attention he tried to gave her may well have rankled him to such an extent that any feelings or loving thoughts turned to hatred. Robert Musgrave, a potman at the *Lord Nelson* said he had heard Slowe say in the bar one night, some seven or eight months before he had killed Mary Hardwick, 'Ill put her – light out one of these days.' Musgrave thought that this was a reference to Miss Hardwick, who apparently did not like serving Slowe and made no particular effort to conceal the fact. Other witnesses said that they had heard Slowe utter threats to Miss

October 3, 1903.   THE ILLUSTRATED POLICE NEWS.   13

BARMAID MURDERED IN WHITECHAPEL.

[SUBJECT OF ILLUSTRATION.]

ANOTHER murder of a barmaid has taken place—this time in a Whitechapel public-house.

The story of the crime was given in evidence before the Worship Street magistrate, when Charles Jeremiah Slowe, twenty-eight years of age, described as a dock labourer, was placed in the dock on a charge of murdering Mary Jane Hardwick in the bar of the Lord Nelson, 296, Whitechapel Road.

With a sprightly step Slowe went into the dock—he has served in the Militia—and listened to the evidence given with his head resting on his left hand. His face bore a serious expression, however.

In formal tones Inspector Collins gave his

had been an eye-witness of the attack upon her sister.

She said she knew the prisoner as an occasional customer. On Wednesday night, at ten minutes past twelve, she saw him enter the house. He came in at the front bar, and Mary Hardwick was looking out of the side door.

He went up to her and struck her right and left. She heard him say. "I've got you now," and witness screamed as she saw him hit her. He hit her with his right fist, and then with his left, but witness did not see what he had in his hand, as he kept his left down.

Witness jumped over the bar and the prisoner ran out. She ran after him, and called out to people not to let him go. Someone caught him, and they brought him back to the house. Witness had run back, and found then that her sister was swooning away.

In reply to the magistrate's clerk, Mrs. Starkey said that she knew the accused man as a customer. She further told the magistrate that she herself had not seen

CHILD MURDERESS.

A Girl of Nine who Threw Boys into the Water.

THE schoolgirl, Florence May Davies, who has been sent to an industrial school by the Middlesbrough magistrates for attempting to drown two little boys in a beck near the Albert Park, has always been a wilful and somewhat extraordinary child.

Of late she has occasioned much trouble at home, and has become totally unmanageable. When before the magistrates she evinced the greatest unconcern, and on being removed repeated the admission she previously made to the police. "I meant to drown both," she said.

She scarcely looks her nine years. She has a bright, intelligent, and merry face, dark hair, and quick, penetrating eyes. She was smartly dressed in black, and seemed incapable of committing the deeds alleged against her.

No specific charge was preferred, the chief constable contenting himself with applying on behalf of the mother for the child's admission to the Roman Catholic Industrial School. The mother keenly supported the application, and added: "Unless she is taken care of, I am afraid something serious will happen."

The first intimation of her daughter's behaviour came to the ears of the mother a fortnight ago, when she was informed that Florence had pushed a little boy into the stream, but had afterwards rescued him. Mrs. Davies administered a severe punishment and kept the girl indoors for ten days. As soon as she was liberated she repeated her strange conduct by decoying an infant three years of age from his home and deliberately pushing him into the same stream. On this occasion she left him to his fate, and he was on the point of being drowned when discovered by a gentleman.

When inquiries were instituted, Florence gave a further exhibition of her unruly behaviour by deliberately cutting up a neighbour's clothes, which were hung out to dry. She also stole 2d. from another girl and spent the money in sweets.

A WILD WEST ADVENTURE.

How Some Desperate Robbers Held up a Train.

MEMORIES of the times of the Wild West have been revived by a daring train robbery just perpetrated outside St. Joseph, Missouri, the robbers rifling the limited mail and getting away with £2,000 in cash.

They are supposed to have boarded the train at St. Joseph, just before it drew out of the station at midnight. The band numbered four, and instead of entering one of the carriages they mounted to the roof, along which they crawled until they came to the parcel car.

Here three of them dropped down to the vestibule, and the fourth continued on to the engine. He covered the driver and the fireman with a pistol in each hand, and ordered them to keep the train moving.

His partners burst into the parcel van, and ordered the four employees there to

BARMAID MURDERED IN WHITECHAPEL.

evidence. He said that shortly after three o'clock in the morning he went to the London Hospital, where he was shown the dead body of a woman with a wound in the chest about as broad as the blade of the knife produced (a large-sized dinner-knife with a blade narrowed for nearly its whole length as if from long use and grinding).

He returned to Bethnal Green Police Station, where the prisoner was detained. Witness charged him with murdering Mary Hardwick by stabbing her with the knife produced. Prisoner made no reply.

The inspector intimated that he would ask for a remand at this point, but the magistrate said there should be something to connect him with the act.

Mrs. Starkey, the deceased girl's sister and landlady of the Lord Nelson, then entered the witness-box. Mrs. Starkey was already dressed in black, and had difficulty in repressing her emotion. She

HOW TO SAVE POUNDS.

A Book of Vital Interest to the Married and those about to Marry, send stamp for postage. R. WALTER, 30, Ilford Road, Ilford Lane, Ilford, Essex.

Slowe earlier in the evening, but she was told that he had been in about eleven o'clock. Except as a customer, she had never seen him speak to her sister.

Inspector Collins told the magistrate that so far as was known there was no motive for the crime.

A week's remand was then ordered, the prisoner being escorted back to the cells.

The murdered girl was an orphan, and a native of Yeadon, near Leeds. For several months she had assisted her sister, who is manageress of the Lord Nelson.

There is no suggestion that Slowe, whose address is given as Rowton House, Whitechapel, was intoxicated.

His mental condition is to be inquired into.

WANDSWORTH GAOL, which is capable of accommodating 1,400 prisoners, is now full, and many of the convicts who are undergoing terms of imprisonment to the extent of two years have been removed to Pentonville and Wormwood Scrubbs. Wandsworth Prison is the largest convict establishment within the metropolitan area.

throw up their hands. Then, while two of the men kept guard, the third rifled the mail parcels, and blew open a small safe with dynamite.

The train was brought to a stop, the robbers mounted horses, and made their escape.

THREE TIMES MARRIED TO THE SAME MAN.

AT Hamilton, Ontario, a curious incident occurred at the funeral of Mrs. Gauld, a woman with a remarkable career. The graveyard is on the top of Beckett's Mountain. While the hearse was going up the hill the coffin slid out and dropped with a crash on the roadway.

Mrs. Gauld enjoyed the unique experience of having been married to the same man three times—first in Scotland, then in Canada, and afterwards on their return to Scotland. It was a runaway match, and the third marriage was to please her parents, who had become reconciled to the husband, who died before her.

Main Picture: Charles Slowe fleeing the public bar of the Lord Nelson after fatally stabbing Mary Hardwick. Miss Hardwick's sister, Mrs Jane Starkey leaps over the bar to go to her younger sister's aid. Top left: Charles Jeremiah Slowe a.k.a Lyons. Top right: Mary Jane Hardwick. The Illustrated Police News

Hardwick, such as, he would 'burn the house down', and that he would knife her, and that someone would have to go through it.

Investigations into Slowe's background revealed that he also used the alias Jeremy Hogan but his real name was in fact Lyons and that his brooding nature was in part caused by his position in life, which unsettled him. An illegitimate child, he was born in Hackney Infirmary. His illegitimacy was a source of great trouble to him. Such was the stigma that he associated with it that, witnesses said that he had told them for that reason he had vowed he would never marry.

On 24 September the *Evening News And Evening Mail* reported:

The Story of the crime was given in evidence before the Worship-street magistrate this forenoon, when Charles Jeremiah Slowe, twenty-eight years of age, described as a dock labourer, was placed in the dock on a charge of murdering Mary Jane Hardwick in the bar of the Lord Nelson, 299 Whitechapel-road.

With a sprightly step Slowe went into the dock – he has served in the Militia – and listened to the evidence given with his head resting on his left hand. His face bore a serious expression, however.

A short but sturdily-built man, with dark, close-cropped hair, and swarthy complexion, he made a far from picturesque figure in the dock. He wore neither collar nor muffler to his blue starched shirt, his black coat was weather-worn, and his boots down at heels.

The *Illustrated Police News* reported on Saturday October 10 1903:

Never having been taught a trade and without steady or regular employment, the prisoner years ago joined the militia, 7th Rifle Brigade, at Dalston. He became colour-sergeant, and at the last annual training, in July, at Bulford Camp, Salisbury Plain, and bore a good character. At ordinary work, however, he seems to have been both unenergetic and irregular.

An inquest held on Friday, 25 September at Stepney Coroner's Court, before Mr Wynne E Baxter, the east London Coroner at which Dr Hudson of the London Hospital stated that Miss Hardwick had received two stab wounds to the chest and that death had been caused by a wound penetrating the right side of the heart. The inquest was adjourned and resumed on Tuesday, 6 October at which the Jury returned a verdict of wilful murder against the accused, who was committed for trial on the Coroner's warrant.

The trial began on Wednesday, 21 October 1903 at the Central Criminal Court, before Mr Justice Bigham. In defence it was argued that there was an absence of premeditation, and that the act was done in such circumstances that the Jury would be justified in reducing the crime to that of manslaughter. Mr Justice Bigham said 'In the eye of the law, if a person used a knife with the intent to do an injury, and death ensued, he was guilty of murder.' After retiring to consider their verdict, the Jury returned after a deliberation of fifteen minutes. They found Slowe guilty of wilful murder. When asked if he had anything to say why sentence of death should not be passed, Slowe made no reply. Before passing sentence of death upon Slowe, Mr Justice Bigham said the Prisoner had been guilty of a cruel and barbarous murder, and he must suffer for the consequences of his act. After sentence of death had been passed, as he was leaving the dock, Slowe said, 'I shall meet it without fear.'

Slowe spent much of his time in the condemned cell singing music-hall songs, apparently unconcerned at his fate. The execution took place at nine o'clock on the morning of Tuesday, 10 November 1903. After what was described by the warders as a restless night, he was wakened at six o'clock and after dressing partook sparingly of breakfast, consisting of eggs, coffee and bread and butter. Afterwards, Slowe spent his time in contemplation with the chaplain. Before leaving the condemned cell, he was given some brandy and water. As he was escorted to the execution shed, Slowe walked with a slightly unsteady gait, but showed no signs of fear. Those present at the execution included Mr Under-Sheriff Metcalfe, acting on behalf of the Sheriff of the County of London, Captain Johnson, the Governor of Pentonville, the prison chaplain, Dr Beamish, and several warders. The executioner was James Billington. Death was instantaneous. Slowe's execution was the fourth to take place at Pentonville since the demolition of Newgate and the first execution there since the public protest by local residents against executions at Holloway and Pentonville.

CHAPTER 18

Vile Murder and Suicide, a Family Wiped Out in Walthamstow

1903

Her throat was slashed from the ear downwards and there were three wounds to her chest.

On Sunday, 27 October 1903, the East End was stunned at the news of the terrible tragedy that had befallen the Marshall family in Walthamstow early that morning.

The Marshall family lived on the ground floor of 89, Griggs Road, Walthamstow. Griggs Road was a road of small, bow-fronted houses, tenanted largely by the artisan class. Clarence John Marshall had once been a chef in fairly good circumstances. He had worked in America for several years, where he had been employed at leading hotels. He moved to Canada for a time before returning to London in 1899. His father said that, after his return from Canada, his son had been very strange, and added that he thought that his mind was affected. Shortly after his return to London he made the acquaintance of his future wife, who was living in comfortable circumstances in Clapton, and they married in 1900, at a Wesleyan church there. They went to live in Woolwich, where Marshall opened a confectionery shop. However, as the shop was not very successful, he gave the business up and went to work in the Arsenal.

In July 1902, having given up his job at the Arsenal, he and his wife moved to Griggs Road, Walthamstow, where their daughter, Elsie, was born in December 1902. Marshall took out a pedlar's certificate in April 1903, since when he had been scraping a living by selling laces and other articles in the street. However, he had been so hard up that he and his family were living chiefly on hand outs from the church he attended.

At a quarter to seven on Sunday morning, a female neighbour of the Marshall's , heard a thud and then a scream, and the scurrying of footsteps in the passage. Through the thin walls that separated the houses came another scream, then the voice of Mrs Marshall shrieking in agony could be heard, as she pitifully called out, 'Oh,

Almighty God – my baby, my baby.' A gurgling sound and a thud followed and then there was silence. A few moments later there was a cry of 'Fire!' People rushed out of their houses and dogs began to bark. There was a crash of glass in the Marshall house and then smoke came billowing out of a broken window.

Mr Friend and some other neighbours from across the road, rushed to the Marshall's house. The front door was locked but a couple of charges at it sent it flying off its hinges. The first man in the smoke-filled passage stumbled across something lying on the floor. He stooped down to see what it was and to his horror discovered it was the body of Mrs Marshall. She lay huddled against the wall, wearing nothing but her nightdress.

Mrs Marshall's face and neck were covered with blood, and there was a gaping hole in her neck. Her throat was slashed from the ear downwards and there were three wounds to her chest. Doctors were soon on the scene but there was nothing they could do as the woman was already dead.

Meanwhile, further discoveries were being made. Mr Friend, who was one of the first to enter the front room said:

Three of us smashed open the bedroom door with some difficulty. We found the room full of smoke, and for a few moments could distinguish nothing, except that there was a roaring fire in the grate, over which a couple of fowls were cooking. In the bow of the window there was another fire, and on the left there was another; and it was very evident that if we had been a minute later the whole house would have been burnt down. But with towels and rugs, and buckets of water we got the fire under [control] just as the brigade rattled up. All of a sudden the thick, stifling smoke cleared a bit, and I could see what awful, horrible work had been going on. It turned me as sick as a dog! There on the hearthrug lay the poor little baby, with its head severed from its body – all but a shred of skin. By the child lay a doll and a bunch of grapes, soaked in blood. On the bed lay Marshall, dead, and smothered with blood. He had cut his own throat, and by his side lay a long, broad-bladed knife. He was only partly dressed – in a shirt, trousers, and a pair of socks.

It was afterwards concluded from what the next door neighbour heard, that Marshall first killed the baby while his wife was out of the room. The child, just ten months old, seems to have been sitting on the hearthrug playing with her doll, while her father was attending to the fowls that were cooking on the fire. There was an open bible in

Main Picture: *Mr Friend and other neighbours break into the bedroom and make a horrific discovery.* **Top right:** *Mrs Marshall, dressed only in her nightdress, lay huddled against the wall.* The Illustrated Police News

the room, with several passages heavily underlined. All around the room were illuminated texts. They were on the walls, on the mantelpiece and even on the door. Above the bed was hung the motto *God is Love*.

During the investigation that followed it became clear that the baby was killed swiftly with one or two savage slashes from her father's big knife, and on entering the room a moment or two afterwards, the child's mother was seized by her husband and flung into the passage, before she was literally hacked to death. It seems that some sort of religious mania could have been the cause of this terrible tragedy. Before he killed himself, Marshall tried to burn the house down. He almost succeeded.

Later that morning, once the news spread of the terrible events in Walthamstow, thousands of people came to Griggs Road to see where the murders had taken place. The morbid curiosity of the general public is seldom easily satisfied and even at ten o'clock that night, there were still several hundred people congregated outside the Marshall's house.

At the inquest, held before Dr Ambrose, Marshall's father, Joseph William Marshall, who after many years working at the Woolwich Arsenal, was receiving a Government pension, gave evidence which suggested that his son was afflicted with homicidal mania; and he added that a brother of the deceased man had murdered his sweetheart, and was subsequently confined in a lunatic asylum, where he died.

Marshall's father said that he did not believe that the couple lived happily together, and that quarrels between his son and daughter-in-law were frequent. He had heard his son threaten to do for his wife but had never seen him show violence towards her.

Several witnesses gave evidence concerning the fire and the discoveries made inside the house. One witness, John Young said that he found a letter on the kitchen table and some coppers. As other people crowded into the room someone picked up the letter and began to read it. Mr Young said he went to fetch water to douse the flames. Unfortunately the letter was lost but Mr Young remembered seeing the words 'No food.'

Mr Charles W Jones, a fireman with the Leyton Fire Brigade, said that when the fire, which was confined to the front room, had been put out, he examined the apartment and found the knife produced, and a doll lying on the hearth rug.

It was also revealed that a quantity of paraffin had been thrown about the room and an empty half-gallon can was found nearby. One witness expressed the opinion that he though that the room had been set on fire before the murders were committed.

Dr Horner gave medical evidence and said that the wounds of the victims were of a shocking character. The murdered woman had several cuts on her arm, breast and neck. The man's injuries were, in the doctor's opinion, self-inflicted. His hair was singed and his hands and face scorched. The baby's skin was also scorched. All three died from hemorrhage, and the wounds were such as would have been caused by the knife produced in evidence.

It was also shown that the family was not without food. A list of articles found on the premises was read out. It included, three duck, two of them cooked, one uncooked, a quantity of bacon, tea, sugar, milk, biscuits, potatoes and butter.

The Coroner, Dr Ambrose, having alluded briefly to the terrible nature of the crime, stated that the evidence was quite clear. The jury returned a verdict 'That Amelia Marshall and her daughter, Elsie, were wilfully murdered by Clarence John Marshall, who afterwards committed suicide, and that at the time Marshall was suffering from a fit of insanity.'

CHAPTER 19

Two Stabbings During Desperate Fighting between Girls in Spitalfields 1903

'You won't hit her, for I'll put this through you.'

Worship Street Police Court heard two cases of stabbing, following extraordinary scenes at a common lodging house in Dorset Street (now Duval Street), Spitalfields, in December 1903, a street with a terrible reputation for violence and murders (associated with the Jack the Ripper murder of Mary Kelly and several other cases including the 1960 murder of Selwyn

The police enter the kitchen of the common lodging house in Dorset Street, to break up the desperate fighting between young women. The Illustrated Police News

EXTRAORDINARY SCENE AT AN EAST-END LODGING HOUSE.
DESPERATE FIGHTING. GIRLS CHARGED WITH STABBING.

Cooney). Prisoners and witnesses were all young girls, and all of them appeared to have been living in the registered lodging house in question. Twenty year old Lottie Scott was charged with stabbing Florence George in the head with a knife. Clara Abbott was charged with stabbing Lottie Scott.

The incident occurred in the communal kitchen of the lodging house, where at about one o'clock in the morning Florence George, Clara Abbot and others were engaged in heated conversation. Clara accused Florence of robbing another girl, named Nellie of 3 shillings, and Florence demanded that Nellie, who was asleep upstairs in bed, be woken and brought downstairs to fight it out.

In her evidence, Nellie said she got out of bed and dressed, but Lottie, who was described as her 'pal', went down first and took up matters on her behalf. Lottie demanded to know what Florrie wanted of Nellie and she responded 'Bring her down.' Lottie replied 'You won't hit her, for I'll put this through you.' It was alleged that Lottie then stabbed Florrie above the eyes. Nellie having arrived on the scene, uproar ensued and the kitchen was full of girls taking sides and fighting and screaming 'murder.' Nellie received a blow in the face from one girl and was dragged down by another. Clara sympathised with Florrie and attacked Lottie, who was then thrown down and crawled under a seat, from where she was dragged up by the hair by Clara and in Lottie's words 'shaken, as a dog shakes a rat.' She afterwards felt a sharp pain in the back and later discovered that she was bleeding.

Three police constables who were called, described the scene as a riot, and one stated that when Lottie Scott and Clara Abbott had been taken in charge for stabbing, the fighting was still going on. Lottie and Clara were committed to the Sessions where they were summarily dealt with.

CHAPTER 20

An Alleged Burglar's Mistake
1903

... he aimed a blow at the woman's head with an iron bar he had secreted in his jacket sleeve.

On Friday, 7 August 1903, a thick-set, determined looking man, named Richard James, living at a common lodging house in Hackney Road, appeared before magistrates at Worship Street Police Court. He was charged with breaking and entering and stealing a gold brooch valued at thirty shillings.

On the night of Saturday, 1 August at about eleven o'clock in the *Cambridge Arms* beer house, St Peter Street, Hackney Road, Mrs Clarke, the landlady, described as a quiet spoken, motherly looking lady, was alone in the bar. She heard a noise in the upper part of the house and went to investigate its cause. On the first landing she found a window was open and there was a ladder leaning against it. She searched the bedrooms on the first floor and was just ascending the flight of stairs to the second floor, when she saw Richard James coming down the stairs. Mrs Clarke called out 'What are you doing?' and James replied, 'Oh, I've made a mistake.' Mrs Clarke then said to him, 'I should think you have made a great mistake.' James stood still and said nothing. Mrs Clarke then said, 'Now then, are you coming down, or shall I come and fetch you?' 'Oh, I'll come down,' James said.

As James came down the stairs Mrs Clarke took hold of him and he struggled to get away from her and attempted to escape through the window by which he had entered the building. As he did so he aimed a blow at the woman's head with an iron bar he had secreted in his jacket sleeve. Fortunately, he missed her and as he was taken off-balance, she took him by the collar and scratched his face. In the ensuing commotion she was able to blow a whistle, which was heard by police, who quickly arrived on the scene. James was arrested and taken away. He was later identified as a notorious ex-convict who had served at least six sentences, his last being five years penal servitude following an appearance at Chelmsford Assizes.

Main Picture: *Mrs Clarke is attacked by a burglar on the first floor landing at the Cambridge Arms.* **Top left:** *Mrs Clarke calls out to the man, 'Now then, are you coming down, or shall I come and fetch you?'* **Bottom left:** *Richard James.* The Illustrated Police News

Sources & Bibliography

Chapter 1: Foul Deeds Through the Ages
The East End Four Centuries of London Life Alan Palmer. John Murray, London (1989)
The East End Nobody Knows Andrew Davies. Macmillan, London (1990)
London's East End Life and Traditions Jane Cox. Weidenfield & Nicolson, London (1994)
Inquests into London and Middlesex Homicides 1673–1782 Thomas R Forbes Pam 14028 The Guildhall Library, London (1976)
The Handbook Guide to London Murder! Horror! .Various. Handbook Publishing Ltd, London (1998)
The History Today Companion to British History Edited by Juliet Gardiner & Neil Wenborn. Collins & Brown, London (1995)
Criminal London Mark Herber. Phillimore (2002)
London Scene from The Strand Gareth Cotterell. Diploma Press, London (1974)

Chapter 2: Foul Deeds within the Precincts of the Tower of London & on Tower Hill
The portion of this chapter concerning Thomas Wentworth Earl of Strafford has been adapted from the author's own work *The Wentworths of Wentworth The Fitzwilliam* [Wentworth] *Estates & The Wentworth Monuments,* published by the Trustees of the Fitzwilliam Wentworth Amenity Trust (2002)
Who's Who in Stuart Britain C P Hill. Shepheard-Walwyn (1988)
The Cambridge Biographical Encyclopedia Second Edition Ed. David Crystal. Cambridge University Press (1998)
Cavaliers and Roundheads Christopher Hibbert. BCA Edition, Harper Collins (1993)
Britain and the Stuarts D L Farmer. G Bell & Sons Ltd, London (1967)
The Stuarts J P Kenyon. Fontana/Collins (1958)
Lord High Executioner Howard Engel. Firefly Books (1996)
The Guinness Guide to Superlative London Paul Murphy. Guild Publishing, London (1989)
London the Mini Rough Guide Rob Humphreys. Rough Guides Ltd, London (2002)

Walking London Andrew Duncan. New Holland (Publishers Ltd.), London (1991)

London's Churches Christopher Hibbert. Macdonald Queen Anne Press (1988)

The Book of Knowledge Ed. Gordon Stowell. The Waverley Book Company Ltd, London (1958) Volumes 1, 4, 7

The Six Wives of Henry Vlll Paul Rival William Heineman Ltd (1937)

The Kings & Queens of England & Scotland Plantagenet Somerset Fry. Guild Publishing (1990)

Chapter 3: Ratcliffe Highway, 1811

The Maul and the Pear Tree T A Critchley & P D James. Constable, London (1971)

Sketches By Boz Charles Dickens Chapter XXl

The Works of Thomas De Quincey – On Murder Considered as one of the Fine Arts and *Postscript* Thomas De Quincey. Adam and Charles Black, Edinburgh MDCCCLXll. The essay first appeared in *Blackwood's Magazine* in February 1827; The *Postscript* was first published 1854

Authentic and Particular Account of the horrid Murders in Ratcliffe Highway and New Gravel Lane Fairburn (1811)

The Fireside Book of Death Robert Wilkins. Robert Hale, London (1990)

Chapter 4: Henry Wainwright and the Murder of Harriet Lane, 1874/5

The Evening Standard, London: Friday 1 October 1875, Saturday, 2 October 1875, Monday, 4 October 1875, Tuesday, 5 October 1875, Wednesday, 6 October 1875, Thursday 7 October 1875, Tuesday, 12 October 1875, Wednesday, 13 October 1875, Thursday, 14 October 1875, Friday, 15 October 1875, Wednesday, 20 October 1875, Monday, 25 October 1875, Tuesday, 26 October 1875, Wednesday, 27 October 1875, Friday, 29 October 1875, Wednesday, 10 November 1875, Saturday, 20 November 1875, Monday, 22 November 1875, Tuesday, 23 November 1875, Wednesday, 24 November 1875, Thursday, 25 November 1875, Friday, 26 November 1875, Saturday, 27 November 1875, Monday, 29 November 1875, Tuesday, 30 November 1875, Wednesday, 1 December 1875, Thursday, 2 December 1875, Friday, 3 December 1875, Monday, 6 December 1875, Friday, 10 December 1875, Monday, 20 December 1875, Tuesday, 21 December 1875.

The Illustrated Police News: Saturday, 27 November 1875, Saturday, 4 December 1875, Saturday, 11 December 1875, Saturday, 18 December 1875, Saturday, 26 December 1875.

The Times: Tuesday, 23 November 1875, Wednesday, 24 November 1875, Thursday, 25 November 1875, Friday, 26 November 1875, Saturday, 27 November 1875, Monday, 29 November 1875, Tuesday, 30 November 1875, Wednesday, 1 December 1875, Thursday, 2 December 1875, Tuesday, 21 December 1875, Wednesday, 22 December 1875.

Notable English Trials The Wainwrights. Edited by H.B. Irving M.A. (Oxon.) with an Appreciation of the Editor by Sir Edward Marshall Hall, K.C. William Hodge & Company, Ltd, Edinburgh and London (1920)

The Chronicles of Newgate Arthur Griffiths. First published 1883. This edition published by Bracken Books, London (1987)

Hangmen of England Horace Bleackley. Chapman and Hall Ltd., London. MCMXXlX

The Old Bailey Stanley Jackson. W.H. Allen, London (1978)

Criminal London Mark Herber. Phillimore & Co Ltd., Chichester (2002)

Chapter 5: Jack the Ripper, 1888

The Crimes Detection and Death of Jack the Ripper Martin Fido. Weidenfield and Nicholson, London (1987)

The New Murderers' Who's Who J H H Gaute and Robin Odell. Harrap Books, Ltd, London (1989)

The Murder Guide Brian Lane. Robinson Publishing Ltd., London (1991)

The Murders of the Black Museum 1870–1970 Gordon Honeycombe. Bloomsbury Books, London (1984)

Murderers' London Ivan Butler. Robert Hale, London (1992)

Murder Guide to London Martin Fido. Grafton Books (1986)

Infamous Murders Various authors. Treasure Press, London (1985)

The Complete Jack the Ripper Donald Rumbelow. W H Allen, (1976)

I Caught Crippen Walter Dew. Blackie, London (1938)

The Times, 8, 10, 24 August, 1, 3, 4, 7, 18, 24, 26 September, 1, 2, 3, 4, 5, 6, 8, 9, 11, 12, 15, 16, 18, 19, 22, 24, 25 October 1888, 10, 12, 13, 14, 16 November 1888

The Star, 1, 3, 5, 8, 10, 12, 15, September, 5, 11, 12, 13, October, 9, 10, 12, 14 November, 12 December 1888

Evening News, 14, 15, 20, 26 September, 1, 4, 10, 17, 20, 31 October, 12, November 8, December 1888
East London Advertiser 14 April, 6, 13, October 1888
The Illustrated Police News 15, 22, 29, September,13 October, 1 December 1888

Chapter 6: Rival Butchers Fight in Whitechapel, 1893
The Illustrated Police News 11 March 1893

Chapter 7: Kidnapping in Bethnal Green, 1893
The Illustrated Police News 20 May 1893

Chapter 8: Coffee-House Keeper Slays His Wife and Stepson, then Shoots Himself, 1893
The Illustrated Police News 3 June 1893

Chapter 9: Tragedy in Hackney Bonfire Night, 1893
The Illustrated Police News 18 November 1893

Chapter 10: William Seaman and the Turner Street Murders, 1896
The Times Saturday 2 May, Thursday 11 June 1896
The Evening News, London, Tuesday 9 June, Wednesday 10 June 1896
The Evening Standard London, Tuesday 9 June, Wednesday 10 June 1896
The Illustrated Police News 11 April, 18 April, 25 April, 9 May, 20 June 1896.
Murder Guide To London Martin Fido. Grafton Books (1986)
The Murders of the Black Museum 1870–1970 Gordon Honeycombe . Bloomsbury Books, London (1984)

Chapter 11: Mysterious Death of a Reputed Bethnal Green Miser, 1897
The Illustrated Police News 2, 23 October 1897

Chapter 12: Garotting in the East End, 1897 & 1899
The Illustrated Police News 4 September 1897, 1 July 1899

Chapter 13: Whitechapel Ruffians Find Their Match, 1897
The Illustrated Police News 6 November 1897

Chapter 14: Suicides
The Illustrated Police News 11 February, 25 November 1899, 15
    August 1903

**Chapter 15: A Mad Cow's Antics Bring Memories of Foul
Deeds Flooding Back, 1899**
The Illustrated Police News 15 April 1899
The East End: Four Centuries of London Life Alan Palmer. John
    Murray, London 1989

**Chapter 16: Edgar Edwards and the Murder of the Darby
Family, 1902**
The Evening News London, Wednesday, 31 December 1902,
    Thursday, 1 January 1903, Friday, 2 January 1903, Saturday, 3
    January 1903, Wednesday, 7 January 1903, Wednesday, 28 January
    1903, Thursday, 29 January 1903, Wednesday 4 February 1903,
    Saturday, 7 February 1903, Thursday, 12 February 1903, Friday,
    13 February 1903, Monday, 16 February 1903, Wednesday, 18
    February 1903, Friday 27 February 1903, Tuesday, 3 March 1903,
    Wednesday, 4 March 1903.
The Times Thursday, 1 January 1903, Thursday, 8 January 1903.
The Illustrated Police News, Saturday 10 January 1903, Saturday, 24
    January 1903, Saturday, 31 January 1903, Saturday 21 February
    1903.
Murder By Gaslight Leonard Piper. Michael O'Mara Books Limited,
    London (1991)

**Chapter 17: Foul Murder in the *Lord Nelson*, Whitechapel,
1903**
The Illustrated Police News 3, 10 October, 14 November 1903

**Chapter 18: Vile Murder and Suicide, A Family Wiped Out In
Walthamstow, 1903**
The Illustrated Police News 3 October 1903

Chapter 19: Two Stabbings during Desperate Fighting Between Girls, In Spitalfields, 1903
The Illustrated Police News 3 December 1898

Chapter 20: An Alleged Burglar's Mistake, 1903
The Illustrated Police News 15 August 1903.

How some commentators viewed huge tracts of the East End, during the Victorian period and early twentieth century. The Illustrated Police News

Index